Writing Ancie

CLASSICAL ESSAYS
Series editor:
Thomas Harrison, University of Liverpool

CLASSICAL ESSAYS

Writing Ancient Persia

Thomas Harrison

Bristol Classical Press

First published in 2011 by
Bristol Classical Press
an imprint of
Bloomsbury Academic
Bloomsbury Publishing Plc
36 Soho Square,
London W1D 3QY, UK
&
175 Fifth Avenue,
New York, NY 10010, USA

CIP records for this book are available from the
British Library and the Library of Congress

ISBN 978 0 7156 3917 7

Picture credit: all the photographs reproduced
in this book are by the author.

Printed and bound in Great Britain by
CPI Antony Rowe, Chippenham and Eastbourne

www.bloomsburyacademic.com

Contents

For Cyrus, Alexander, Alfred and Flora

The real fact is, young Europe is whipped and schooled into admiration of Greece, till no one dares give a candid opinion. Otherwise, how can men in their senses affect to believe all that stuff about the invasion of Xerxes?

Edward Eastwick (1864: 26-7)

Acknowledgements

This is an essay about the writing of the history of the Achaemenid Persian empire. It is not itself a history of Achaemenid Persia (let alone of other periods of ancient Persian history), or even a prelude to the writing of one, but a discussion of the way in which such histories have been, are being, and might be, written. Achaemenid history is now a vast scholarly field – one in which, by rights, as Heleen Sancisi Weerdenburg once put it, 'one should be thoroughly acquainted with at least six ancient languages' and their associated scholarly literatures (1990: 253). I might as well state clearly now: I do not pretend to this ideal. What follows is the account of a Greek historian. This is not as perverse as it might seem, given the centrality of Greek sources for Persian history. Indeed, much as one can only be awed by the splendour, scale and variety of so much past and current Achaemenid scholarship, it is an underlying principle of this book that Hellenists can and must engage with this body of work. This essay also makes no pretence of being exhaustive in its coverage. In particular, it focuses on the early period of Achaemenid history in which Persian sources are more plentiful and Herodotus' *Histories* constitute the main Greek body of evidence. Certain themes, regions, classes of evidence, and indeed modern scholarship, central to a full historiography of the Achaemenid Persian world receive little or no attention: the reader will look largely in vain for discussion of Persian religion, for example (apart from the theme of 'religious tolerance'), for the details of Persian satrapal administration, or for the modern Iranian reception of Achaemenid history. I hope that these and other exclusions are, at least in part, defensible in terms of my focus on the overall shape and tendency of recent narratives; I have little doubt, however, that they are also driven by the limits of my expertise.

In daring to undertake a critique of a scholarly field in which I have only a toehold, I have also necessarily relied upon the generosity and expertise of others. Tom Holland, Lloyd Llewellyn-Jones, Kostas Vlassopoulos, and, not least, my Liverpool colleague Christopher Tuplin have all read and commented on a full draft – and, though they cannot be held responsible for the remaining errors and eccentricities, have both helped me to refine my thinking and saved me from embarrassment. The ideas expressed here have been tested both by audiences of scholars (not least through the Mediterranean and Near Eastern Studies programme of Trinity College Dublin) and by generations of excellent students at St Andrews and at Liverpool. The experience of working with Deborah Blake and her colleagues at Duckworth has, as always, been a delight. My research has been assisted enormously by the award by the Leverhulme Trust of a Philip Leverhulme Prize. And the support of Catherine Pickstock, in what was otherwise a difficult period, was essential to my completing this essay (and to much else). I should like to express my heartfelt gratitude to all of these, and – not least – to the individual historians of Persia who feature so prominently in this volume, not only for the scholarship to which I am responding, but in the case of Amélie Kuhrt for her encouragement and kindness during a period I spent as a British Academy postdoctoral fellow in her department.

Finally, Frances Harrison, Kasra and Cyrus Naji looked after and fed me royally during a trip to Iran in 2007. It is to Cyrus, and to his cousins, that this book is dedicated.

A *note to the reader*

In order to make the book accessible to more than the initiated, I have in general avoided all abbreviations, e.g. of the names of ancient authors, or of journals. Persian royal inscriptions are cited by the standard abbreviations used in e.g. Kent 1953 or Lecoq 1997. Fragmentary Greek historians are cited according to the system of Jacoby's *Die Fragmente der griechischen Historiker* (now progressively being re-edited and translated as part of a project known as *Brill's New Jacoby*), according to which, for example, 688 F 1 denotes Ctesias fr. 1. Kuhrt 1997 is a readily available source of the most important texts, with excellent notes. The site of Darius' inscribed account of his accession I have spelled consistently as Behistun; this is the same place as Bisitun.

Preface

We thus see an empire which included the whole of the known world and a good deal of territory then unknown, which stretched from the burning sands of Africa to the icebound borders of China, vast but obedient.

P.M. Sykes (1915: i.180)[1]

So one writer – from the height of Britain's imperial age, and with something of a nostalgic glow – described the Achaemenid Persian empire. So-called from its ruling dynasty, the Achaemenid empire was founded by Cyrus in the mid-sixth century BC and toppled through the rampaging conquests of Alexander the Great in the late fourth. Its influence has been much longer-lasting, however. Not only did later Iranian rulers look back to the Achaemenids, with the Sassanian kings placing their tombs alongside those of Darius and Xerxes, for example, or through the comic pageantry that the last Shah orchestrated for the anniversary of Cyrus in 1971.[2] The Achaemenid empire has also provided a model for others: most famously, Cyrus' statement of his settlement with the Babylonians in the so-called Cyrus Cylinder has been commonly (mis)interpreted as the first universal declaration of human rights.[3]

The empire of the Achaemenids is, of course, not the uncomplicated historical entity that it is sometimes presented as. Though the Great Kings had a formidable central control of the provinces (or 'satrapies') of their empire, their rule like that of any ancient empire was inevitably something of a patchwork, with some more mountainous and inhospitable territory tied to them more tenuously, through little more than the acts of allegiance of tribal chiefs, than the cultivated plains.[4] The boundaries of the empire fluctuated over time: Egypt, for example, fell out of their grasp for significant stretches of the fourth century BC. As for the geographical extent of the Persian empire, the empire covered much more than just the modern boundaries of modern Persia or Iran, as my opening quotation describes.

The chronological bounds of the Achaemenid empire are also at issue. Herodotus' story of Cyrus' birth and rise to kingship in Book I of his *Histories* assumes that, at the time of Cyrus' birth, Persia was under the rule of the kings of Media. It is pretty clear, however, that though Persia may have been, in some way, a vassal state of neighbouring kingdoms before Cyrus, it was a state of some sort. The opening declaration of the Cyrus Cylinder (written in Akkadian) shows Cyrus not only projecting the extent of his rule, but also his lineage:[5]

I, Cyrus, king of the world, mighty king, king of Babylon, king of Sumer and Akkad, king of the four quarters, son of Cambyses, great king, king of Anshan, grandson of Cyrus, great king, king of Anshan, great-grandson of Teispes, great king, king of Anshan ...

A significant question mark also hangs over the continuity of the Achaemenid dynasty. More than any other of the kings, it was Darius who insisted on his status as an Achaemenid, but this was in fact a response to his dubious claim to the throne. The circumstances are extraordinarily complex and peculiar, but it seems highly likely that he usurped the throne from the brother of Cambyses (Bardiya in Persian, Smerdis in Greek), and then made out that Cambyses' brother had in fact been a lookalike impostor (with only the crucial distinguishing feature, in the Greek account of Herodotus, that he had no ears[6]). Darius may have been related to Cyrus, but it is clear (not least from the fact that his father and grandfather were alive at the time of his accession) that his kingship did not derive primarily from birth. It is also clear that he went to extraordinary lengths to project his legitimacy. His account of his accession was inscribed in three languages high on a steep mountainside at Behistun, and sent in further copies to all corners of the empire (whence it made its way, in distorted fashion, onto the pages of Herodotus' *Histories*).[7] He also recruited Cyrus retrospectively into his narrative: 'I am Cyrus, the king, an Achaemenid', an Old Persian inscription proclaims at Cyrus' royal palace of Pasargadae[8] – though the writing of Old Persian in cuneiform script was an innovation of Darius'. In short, as one distinguished archaeologist of the period has written, 'the changes that Darius introduced when he came to the throne were probably far more drastic than has hitherto been realized'.[9]

There is also, finally, some discussion even over the ending point of the Achaemenid empire – though this is more of a debating point. The histories of Alexander provide some of the best evidence for the Persian empire in the period leading up to his conquests. Alexander did not simply throw over all aspects of Persian administration, but of necessity adopted many of them, just as he took over some aspects of Persian royal clothing so as to project himself plausibly as a king demanding respect. (Though he burned down Darius' palace of Persepolis, the administrative centre of the empire, as a grand gesture of his desire for vengeance for the Persian wars 150 years before, he seems to have done so only reluctantly and after a considerable delay.[10]) For this reason he has been dubbed – in some ways, perversely – the 'last of the Achaemenids'.[11] Much of the impetus for the study of the Achaemenid empire indeed has derived from the study of Alexander's successors. The question of how much of their practice derived from pre-existing Near Eastern practices led a number of scholars to go back and see what evidence there was,[12] to attempt to locate the Achaemenid period within a longer flow of Near Eastern history, rather than seeing it either as an anomaly or as the last phase of a tired 'Oriental' monarchy brutally ruptured by an Alexander who was 'un mélange de Cecil Rhodes et du Général Gordon'.[13] Increasingly also it has become evident that the Achaemenid empire did not emerge from a cultural void, but was itself shaped by the experience of previous Near Eastern kingdoms, not least that of Elam.[14]

So the Achaemenid empire is a more complex, more unsettled entity than its mere identification as one of the great empires of the ancient world might suggest. This is also true for another reason: the shifting of modern scholarly (and indeed more popular[15]) interpretations. Unlike the study of

Greek history (often envisaged as a process of filling in gaps, or of building on earlier foundations, with only occasional currents of revisionism), the recent study of Achaemenid Persia is founded on an imagined break with past scholarship and past understanding. The history of ancient Persia has, indeed, to a substantial extent *been rewritten* in the last thirty years, not least by the international group of scholars associated with the Achaemenid History Workshops. These colloquia – initiated by Heleen Sancisi-Weerdenburg in 1980, and then carried on by her, Amélie Kuhrt and others[16] – brought together individuals from a variety of backgrounds: some trained as archaeologists or in Assyriology or biblical studies, as well as 'renegade' classicists, liberating themselves from their intellectual formation.[17] Inevitably there were differences in approach: 'discussion, more than agreement, is the main aim of these workshops', in Sancisi-Weerdenburg's words.[18] Many of the scholarly trends of the workshop can be traced in the preceding years: scholars such as Root, Sancisi-Weerdenburg and Briant all began their studies independently of one another, and from very different starting points.[19] And much progress was made independently of the annual meetings.[20] (The open model of workshops was chosen indeed as the 'best available alternative', because financially viable, to that – proposed by Briant – of 'integrated research units'.[21]) With all these caveats, however, the workshops both created a tight-knit scholarly team and wrought a transformation in attitudes to the topic of study – a rare example of a group of scholars adding up to more than the sum of their parts. In the words of Pierre Briant, looking back from the vantage point of his monumental *History of the Persian Empire*, 'now I could join the "Achaemenid community", which, small in number, offers the inestimable advantage of being international and linked by bonds of friendship'.[22] Or, as Sancisi-Weerdenburg put it in 1990, 'a new picture of the empire is gradually emerging', a picture not just of a series of royal life stories, but 'in which some of the structures that connected the imperial summit with the day-to-day life of the subjugated populations has become visible'.[23]

How have these scholars rewritten Persian history? First, through a great deal of patient, careful work. Just as Greek history relies, more than is often made explicit, on the groundwork done (not without flair) by early German scholars, so some of the major works of the new wave of Achaemenid history – most notably, Briant's history – provide the kind of exhaustive discussion of events or themes (the succession of x or y king, or the royal dinner, say) that will inevitably be a point of reference for many years.[24] Briant has himself admitted, disarmingly, that 'from the moment I began this undertaking, I was stuck with a sort of encyclopedism, with all the risks and illusions that go with this approach'.[25] (It is somehow characteristic that a classical historian with whom apparently Briant feels a particular affinity should be Polybius, renowned likewise for his systematic approach.[26])

Secondly, through the introduction of new material. In particular, new histories have brought to the fore the so-called 'treasury' and (much more numerous) 'fortification' texts from Persepolis, administrative records (details, predominantly, of the storage and distribution of the agricultural produce of the region surrounding Persepolis) which were recorded on clay tablets, stored, and then (in the case of the treasury tablets, at least) baked when Alexander torched Persepolis as a symbol of Persian power.[27] The work of editing these texts, establishing their underlying scribal conventions, and painstakingly interpreting them – and reconstructing the Elamite language in which they were, for the most part, written – is indeed a parallel story to the one treated here: a heroic narrative, lasting decades and by no means completed, in which a small group of outstanding scholars (not least, George Cameron and Richard Hallock) worked patiently together in spite of seemingly insurmountable obstacles of geographical distance or the interruptions of war.[28] The careful unpicking of these texts, coupled with a new emphasis on *structures*,[29] has led to an understanding of the administration of the Persian empire – the rations supplied to leading Persians, or the way in which the system of royal roads and couriers was organised – that would be impossible merely from Greek sources.[30]

Finally, however, the revision of Persian history has been the result of a new approach to Greek sources, and a reaction against the narratives derived from them: a desire to 'break away from the dominant Hellenocentric view' as Heleen Sancisi-Weerdenburg put it in her introduction to the first volume of the workshop's proceedings, 'to dehellenise and decolonialise Persian history', as she put it more graphically,[31] and somehow to launder the pejorative bias of classical Greek sources – inevitably the basis of much of any modern reconstruction of Achaemenid Persia. Whereas the traditional narratives (to distil slightly the version given of them[32]) saw the Persian empire as neutered and decadent in the wake of the Greek-Persian wars, only waiting for Alexander to deliver the fatal blow 150-odd years later, the new Achaemenid historians place the emphasis instead on the resilience of the Achaemenid empire and on the tolerance and pragmatism of its rulers. Out go the stereotypes of Achaemenid kings and queens as Oriental despots – of mad king Cambyses' depredations in Egypt or of the cruel punishments of Amestris, wife of Xerxes – and in their place emerge more moderate and less colourful figures: royal wives dedicated to the interests of their male relatives, or a Cambyses in line with his father Cyrus as a 'builder of empire'.

It is this revolution in the understanding of Achaemenid Persia that is the topic of this essay. The success of this academic programme[33] can be measured by the 2005 British Museum exhibition, 'Forgotten empire', which in general might be said to have enshrined (and brought to a wider audience) the conclusions of recent work.[34] Like any scholarly consensus, however, the new Achaemenid historiography gives rise to almost as many further questions as it settles. Is it really legitimate to launder Greek sources – or to 'decode' them[35] – as breezily as is sometimes done? Are previous narratives of Persian history really so monochrome in their perspective? And what other perspectives, other questions, are being occluded by current scholarly concerns? Much of what follows is taken up with critique, with exploring the tensions within or between recent scholarly opinions. But it is hoped that this essay, and the reader, will not lose sight either of the reality of the Persian empire which is ultimately the object of study, or of the achievement of those scholars – both recent and longer ago – who have done so much to uncover it.

1

Against the Grain

In reading the classical authors, we must distinguish the
Greek interpretative coating from the Achaemenid nugget of information. Rejecting the interpretation the
Greek writers gave to an Achaemenid court custom does
not imply that the custom or practice they were dealing
with was pure and simple invention on their part.

Pierre Briant (2002: 256)

How do we get close to understanding the reality of Achaemenid Persia? Still harder, how can we elicit the Persians' own
version of events, their own perspective? The study of Achaemenid Persian history presents a rare kind of puzzle: like the
study of archaic Greek history, with its decoding of scattered
bits of evidence from a later period,[1] the object of study can
only be reconstructed from – and in a sense may only be
constituted by – a whole range of different perspectives: those of
the Greek (and other) subjects of Persian imperialism, the administrative records of Persepolis, and the grandiloquent pronouncements of the early Persian kings, especially Darius and Xerxes.

All these main sources of evidence have their limitations (of
knowledge or of scope); all of them *shape* their reader's views
according to their own agendas. To begin with the Greek

19

sources, though the Persians undoubtedly made a vivid impression on the memories of the Greeks of the Persian war period, and though a small number of individual Greeks (such as the fourth-century doctor Ctesias of Cnidus) may have had experience of the Persian court, direct experience of Persians or Persia was very rare. We are often forced into surmising what the possible route for information may have been – guessing for example that the Herodotean version of Cambyses as a mad tyrant is the product of hostile Egyptian (or Persian) sources. Clear traces of Persian administrative records or of Persian royal ideology do survive in Greek sources. (Indeed it will be a recurrent theme, throughout this essay, that some Greek writers understood Persia much better than they are sometimes given credit for.) Herodotus' catalogues of the Persian empire and of the Persian army, for example, or his account of Darius' accession, clearly derive in part from Persian records (the latter from Behistun), even if he may have moulded them to Greek models or even introduced elements from Greek predecessors such as Hecataeus;[2] the King's self-fashioning as a kind of global policeman sorting out the petty squabbles of his subject peoples also finds reflection in Greek accounts, in descriptions (spoken by or to Persian characters) of the futility of warfare among the Greeks.[3]

The distortion that Persian society or Persian ideology undergoes in the Greek sources can take a number of shapes. It cannot adequately be understood as some kind of generalised pejorative coating. Distortion can be the result of a variety of Greek ideological agendas, the need for Persia to provide an exemplum of moral decadence (or of benign monarchy), or to create a tidy narrative of decline from the austere heyday of the elder Cyrus.[4] Persian material is also subject to exactly the same 'deformation' that affects other oral sources, for example for the history of the archaic Greek world:[5] the preservation of the sensational in preference to the merely accurate, or the introduction of error and confusion without any underlying ideological direction. Where the deformation of Persian material arguably differs, however, is in the lack of controls on distortion: where an oral account of contemporary Athenian or Theban society would have been circumscribed by (some knowledge of) the historical reality, it is easy to imagine that accounts of Persia might have been limited primarily by their relationship to an easily recognisable stereotype.[6] (The fact that the material on ancient Persia that survives in Greek sources must represent only a small share of that which circulated, say, in the aftermath of the Persian wars, makes it easy to underestimate Greek 'knowledge' of Persia or the extent to which Greek writers may have manipulated their versions of Persian institutions.[7]) Even where an author has witnessed Persian society at close hand, such autopsy is not the panacea for inherited prejudice that one might have hoped. Though Xenophon, on the back of his encounter with the heartland of the Persian empire in the course of the revolt of Cyrus the Younger, preserves many details of Persian etiquette, for example, in his *Anabasis*, his modelling of Cyrus the Elder as the ideal of the monarch, and his denunciation of the subsequent decline in Persian society, in the *Cyropaedia* show how easily such experience can be subordinated, even by an exemplary witness, to other concerns than accurate portrayal. The philosophical ends of the work may well trump its Persian setting; Xenophon's main concern in regard to the Persian 'décor' of the *Cyropaedia* may have been to ensure that it was sufficiently (but not excessively) alien to his Greek readership.[8]

Greek sources thus offer a variety of oblique perspectives on Persia. What is perhaps less immediately obvious is the partial nature (in both senses of the word 'partial') of the Persian sources. It is more than a debating point to observe that no category of Persian material provides unmediated access to the reality of Achaemenid Persia. The surviving Persepolis texts present problems all of their own: they date exclusively from the late sixth and early fifth centuries BC (and disproportionately from a much smaller range of years); they primarily concern the region surrounding Persepolis, rather than the empire at large; and they are written (at least, the vast majority are written) in Elamite, 'a very strange language', much of the terminology of which is obscure.[9] (The number of fortification texts edited to date may, it has been calculated, represent only five per cent of the texts produced in Persepolis in the years in question, raising the possibility that whole classes of material are missing from our picture.[10]) As we will see, the Persian kings, in their iconography as in their inscribed pronouncements (which relate closely to one another) borrow motifs from previous Near Eastern kingdoms: Persian kingship and Persian power are presented as the summation of previous empires.[11] The emphasis of Persian iconography, or of Persian royal inscriptions, on calm and stability means that only the slightest differences can be discerned between kings; the timeless presentation of the inscriptions makes it near-impossible to distinguish concrete events from eternal truths.[12] Our one Persian narrative, on the other hand – Darius' account of his accession as inscribed at Behistun – is markedly problematic, even by the standards of the accounts of Herodotus or Ctesias.[13] In the words of Christopher Tuplin, 'Darius did not buy into historiography and then buy out of it again ...: he never bought into it in the first place'.[14]

Arguably, indeed, the Persian sources present more of a mirage than the Greek. The Greek accounts are filled with contradictions and fissures; as a result, they undercut their own narratives. Herodotus, for example, can perpetuate the Greek idea that the Persians worshipped their rulers – through retelling a stirring episode in which two Spartans refused to make a gesture of submission (known as *proskynesis*) to the King – while at the same time seeming to reveal that he knew better, that it was no more than the greeting expected of one man to his social superior.[15] The Persian sources, by contrast, studiedly sustain the same impression. One American visitor to Persia in 1929 memorably complained of the monotony and formalism of the sculptures of Persepolis, and of the 'bored composure' with which the Great King plunges 'a dagger into rampant unicorns and lions and griffins' (see Fig. 1).[16]

[F]inally you tire of the twelve hundred human figures that adorn these ruins and file in such stiff and endless procession to do honour to the monarch. Who was this fellow, anyway, about whom all the world so solemnly paraded? No deeds, no joy, no life, but what his whim decreed.

We now know that the precise repetition of some features of

Fig. 1. Persepolis: royal hero in combat with bird-headed monster, Hall of a Hundred Columns, north doorway in west wall.

the Persepolis sculptures – details of hair or ears, for example – were no accident: the sculptors at the site operated in teams, all working to a central blueprint (see Fig. 2).[17] We also now appreciate – especially since one of the masterpieces of the new Achaemenid historiography, Margaret Cool Root's *King and Kingship in Achaemenid Art* – that the repetition and formalism of the Persepolitan sculptures was an integral part of what one might term the Kings' artistic programme, one which mapped neatly onto the ideological messages of the royal inscriptions. 'Stylistic vigour and the dynamism of ephemeral encounters and fleeting charisma have no place in the canon of Achaemenid art', as Root puts it memorably;[18] instead the accent is on a 'sense of placidity, of refinement, of ordered control' (see Fig. 3). Mythic beasts are wrestled into submission; the followers of the Lie are confounded; and peoples all troop in order in inevitable homage to their King, their convergence symbolising the wholeness of the empire itself (see Figs 4-5).[19] In Root's concluding words:[20]

> The world is at peace on the walls of Persepolis as it never was in actuality. While news of the Persian sack of Miletus was striking terror in the Athenian soul, artisans from near and far were carving dreams in stone for Darius. It is easy to be cynical about this paradox between the actuality and the art of the Pax Persiana. And yet, even to have conceived this *vision* of an imperial cosmos where the Four Quarters sing harmonious praises to the power of the king was something unprecedented in the ancient world: a haunting finale to the pre-Hellenic East.

What the Persian sources give us, in other words, is not (for the most part) a secure check against the Greeks' representations of Persia, but potent images, representations of their own. How then are we to marry them, as best we can, to

Fig. 2. Persepolis: detail of the Apadana relief.

Fig. 3. Persepolis: the King and attendants (with parasol) from the palace of Xerxes, east doorway.

1. *Against the Grain*

Fig. 4: Persepolis: Bactrian delegation from the east staircase of the Apadana.

Fig. 5. Persepolis: relief of the King in audience, formerly the centrepiece of the reliefs of the Apadana.

provide the most satisfying account of Persian history? The first point to emphasise is simply that, in the often-repeated mantra of Pierre Briant, we cannot choose our sources – and we cannot choose to disregard any class of source material. 'We have no choice but overwhelming reliance on Greek historiography to reconstruct a narrative thread', as he puts it.[21] And indeed the Persian historian is caught in an uncomfortable bind: relying on Greek sources – sometimes, it seems, almost resentfully – while working against their grain.

This discomfort is reflected in the pejorative terms in which the main Greek sources are described, which (from the perspective of a Greek historiographer at least) tend to focus on what writers do *not* do, and arguably *could not* be expected to do, rather than on what they do. So Xenophon's *Anabasis*, his priceless account of his own role in the revolt of Cyrus the Younger against his brother, is damned with faint praise as 'lively, adventuring … a fully coloured careerist memoir suffused with exploratory and military ideology, rather than a logistical guide to the Persian empire'.[22] Likewise Herodotus, though he can be given credit for his 'intellectual generosity' or for not being more black and white in his views on foreign peoples,[23] is referred to as 'our most garrulous informant', 'the Cecil B. de Mille of ancient history' (and the author of an 'elaborate dynastic soap opera'), and yet, surprisingly for such an apparently incontinent author, one who showed more attention when indulging in satire of the Persian court: 'he focussed with great precision on a vivid but highly satirical presentation of the Persian king and court', and was 'adept at parodying themes of Eastern kingship'.[24] More praise indeed seems to be reserved for those historians deemed, we can suspect, to be more easily minable, or to have less of an agenda of their own. The Alexander histories 'constitute ... an "Achaemenid" source of exceptional interest, once they have been decoded';[25] late sources such as Aelian or Polyaenus receive surprisingly attentive focus.[26]

These characterisations of the main Greek sources are often strikingly at variance with those of recent scholarship within Greek historiography. Though Briant may acknowledge that Herodotus 'shows no evidence of systematic hostility to the Persians',[27] this is a world away from the shaded accounts of Herodotean ethnography (and of the invention of the barbarian more broadly) that have been produced in the last decades.[28] Briant's passing description of the close of the *Histories* as 'an abrupt end' again reflects ignorance of much of the most important Herodotean scholarship with its focus on narrative.[29] And, especially in his earlier work perhaps, Briant shows a confidence in the identification of Herodotus' Persian or Egyptian sources that few would share now.[30] Who can read everything? The Achaemenid historian has quite enough bibliographically to contend with as it is. But the absence of some prominent works in these fields from the bibliographies of Achaemenid historians seems to reflect a broader blind spot: a lack of concentration on historical accounts as narrative, a narrow approach to 'bias',[31] and a tendency to judge ancient historians by an anachronistic set of expectations.

To begin from the last point, Achaemenid historians are inclined to criticise Greek authors for not providing what they (the modern historians) need. So, for example, Briant condemns Herodotus for treating Darius' Scythian expedition 'only very superficially' (on the basis of a 'narrowly Helleno-centric orientation'),[32] or for presenting 'what we consider the important causes of a historical event ... in a personal, anec-dotal form'.[33] This kind of criticism seems to assume an identity of approach between Herodotus and the modern historian, that we can fairly judge an ancient historian by our own professional standards. As Tim Rood has successfully argued in defence of Thucydides' allegedly 'sketchy' narrative of the fifty years after the Persian wars, the *Pentacontaetia*, accusations of superficiality often betray false expectations: we forget to ask what a historian is himself setting out to do.[34] When Briant places the emphasis on Herodotus' differences, the suspicion of anachronistic standards is in fact confirmed. 'The problem, obviously, is that Herodotus clearly does not ask the questions to which historians seek answers', as he puts it in the context of the Ionian revolt against Persian rule.[35] But this is not a statement of the fundamental differences between Herodotus' historical understanding and our own, of his (to our minds) alien preconceptions as well as aims in writing 'history', but rather a statement that he has fallen short, that he has failed to *ask the questions that he should*.

The reason for objecting to the term 'bias' as applied to ancient sources is that it runs the risk of suggesting that a historian's position can so straightforwardly be identified: that, but for a hostility to city x or a soft spot for city y, he is a colleague. The centrality of personalities to ancient historical texts, for example, may simply be the result of a deliberate choice on the part of the historian (the desire, to put it negatively, to focus on personal tittle-tattle rather than to take a more considered approach to historical causation); or it may be, to an extent at least, the result of the greater influence of individuals in the events described; or it may, more fundamentally, be the function of a very different conception of what matters in historical causation.[36] This last possibility might easily be seen as a euphemism for the primitive nature of historical explanation in Greek historiography, as justifying the absence of causation. However, the way in which Herodotus accumulates the personal triggers for the Persian wars systematically, making sure to follow them up in his narrative, suggests that it reflects a more considered approach.

The difference can be illustrated by taking the example of a single individual who was (in Herodotus' account, at least) crucial in bringing Greece and Persia closer to conflict: the Greek doctor at the Persian court, Democedes of Croton. Democedes' story is a convoluted one.[37] Originally taken prisoner as part of the entourage of Polycrates of Samos, his expertise led to his rising to prominence in the Persian court – although (as with other Greeks in the Persian court, at least within the narrative of Greek accounts[38]) he always nursed the desire to return to his homeland. After successfully treating a tumour in the breast of Darius' wife Atossa, he saw his opportunity and asked for a favour in return. At his instruction, Atossa approached Darius in bed, and coaxed him ('You have so much power, but you do nothing with it') to show the Persians that they were ruled by a man by attacking the Greeks. This led to Democedes' being sent on a scouting expedition to the Mediterranean, from which he absconded – but only after making a dig at Darius that presumed the King's familiarity with Greek wrestling.[39] For Briant, the purpose of the Democedes affair is to 'show that the Persian Empire and

31

the Greek world were becoming acquainted well before the onset of the Persian Wars and that, quite early on, Darius cherished notions of conquest in the west'.[40] The personal focus of the episode can be sloughed off as a carrier for the historical lesson it contains. But this is to miss the historiographical context, and to read the episode too quickly from the perspective of the rationalising modern historian. Democedes is one of a series of individuals who, for narrow and selfish ends of their own, progressively enmesh the Greek world and the Persian court to the point where war becomes inevitable: Syloson of Samos, for example, or Aristagoras or Histiaeus of Miletus. The broader historical judgement that Persia and Greece were coming into increasing contact is unobjectionable, though we might want to give a greater emphasis to the role of Greek initiative,[41] but the fact that these individuals cannot see the larger pattern, the fact that there are inadvertent consequences to their actions: these are some of the messages of Herodotus' account.[42]

What this example makes clear is the need to read any particular episode within its position in the narrative more broadly, to consider what work any episode is doing within the text itself before we distil its use as a historical source. The same principles and the same dangers apply, of course, in the context of any historical question – in using Greek historical sources, say, for the writing of archaic history – but when one takes into account the apparent lack of sympathy felt by Achaemenid historians for Greek sources, the risk of bad historical readings is magnified. How should we do it instead? Briant, in fact, provides a good general manifesto. 'However partisan and ideological a Greek text may be, when it is *located in the web of its associations*, it can provide a stimulating Achaemenid reading'.[43] The difficulty consists in following through on this manifesto, and in the complexity of the web of associations of any one episode (which talk of historical 'nuggets' or of 'decoding' grossly underestimates[44]).

Another example – the story of Deioces, the inventor in Herodotus' histories of the Median kingship[45] – brings out many of the difficulties. For Briant, this episode is treated simply in black-and-white terms of factual accuracy:

> Herodotus' Median tale is highly suspect. To be sure, the historicity of the kings depicted is hard to deny, and there is no compelling reason to doubt their chronology, but the story of the reforms imposed by Deioces resembles an existing model of the 'founding father' too closely for us to place blind confidence in it. Furthermore, the institutions set up by Deioces (capital, personal guard, audience ritual, Eyes and Ears of the king) are strangely similar to the Achaemenid institutions frequently described by the Greek authors, so much so that we are tempted to think that Herodotus ... applied (or could have applied) what he knew of the Persian court practices of his own day as a veneer over an entirely imaginary Media.[46]

What's wrong with this? If Herodotus is not an accurate Polybian historian, there is it seems only one alternative: that he is a cynical inventor of a plausible narrative (in the mould of Detlev Fehling and the so-called 'Liar School'[47]). (Similarly, Sancisi-Weerdenburg – in another context – makes arguably too firm a contrast between 'literature that was *meant* to add something to the knowledge about Persia and writings that use the already available knowledge for other purposes'.[48]) Even if we accept (as I do) that the description of Deioces is coloured, suffused by Achaemenid 'knowledge', there is no reason to assume that this was a painstakingly constructed collage of Herodotus'. For a start, much as we may not want simply to pass on the responsibility for Herodotean logoi to his sources, it seems unquestionable that Herodotus moulded a pre-existing logos (whether an oral tradition or a report of a Babylonian archive[49]) to his own purposes: it is clear in other words that there are *limits* to his invention. The identification of the story as, most likely, an oral logos should also direct us to its *moral* dimension.[50] It reads indeed as if it were a kind of parable of kingship. The society from which Deioces' rule emerges is one without any social order. Like the story of Psammetichus' rise to kingship in Egypt (from a position in which he was one of twelve regional chieftains),[51] the story of Deioces may suggest the moral that in Asia monarchy is inevitable (look, if you leave them alone in a kind of experiment, this is what happens!); like other episodes from Herodotus' gallery of Egyptian kings, it also clearly explores the tensions within kingship – whether, or how, the just man can remain just as a king (or how he ensures that his just rule is followed).[52] The pattern of the retrojection of Achaemenid details onto Deioces which Briant detects is part of a much broader pattern of analogy within the *Histories*: so, for example, the mirroring of Darius' Scythian expedition and the Athenians' resistance to the Persian invasions, or the analogy between Persian and Trojan wars.[53] It is not simply then that Deioces is portrayed as an Achaemenid but that he is cast as an archetype of (Asian?) kingship in general.

Relying on such accounts then, either for the basic shape of a narrative or for historical details contained within them, becomes more problematic the more one appreciates the complexity of their ideological colouring (and the more complex their engagement with pre-existing narrative traditions[54]). There is an illuminating parallel here with the use of later sources for the reconstruction of archaic Greek history. A traditional approach to the sources for, say, the tyrannies of archaic Athens or Corinth, was to take the major account and fillet it of evidently implausible details: miracles of pots boiling without any heat being applied, or anecdotes of Odyssean trickery which look like later embellishments.[55] As Christiane Sourvinou-Inwood argued, however, this importantly underestimates the extent to which such logoi are 'articulated in a mythological idiom'.[56] The very shape of a story, the basic narrative, can be spun out of an idea: so, for example, the story of the attempt at tyranny of the Athenian Peisistratus – with his being carried into town by a girl dressed as Athena – may be the distorted end-product of an original idea of his divine favour.[57] (Similarly, as Dominique Lenfant has suggested in another context, the very idea of Persian luxury and its 'association with ruin' can itself prompt 'a supposedly historical proposition'.[58]) This then limits the type of history that one can hope to write, shifting the focus from the reconstruction of events and institutions to the mapping of ideologies and representations.

This has serious implications for the type of use to which Greek sources are put by Persian historians. The reconstruction of many elements of Persian history is achieved by constructing a kind of collage of ancient sources. So, for example, if he wants to gain an understanding of the protocols that governed access to the King, the historian will harvest anecdotes and 'nuggets' from a chronologically scattered range of sources. This strategy may be desirable on other grounds: it may help, for example, to trace common narrative patterns across authors and periods, or to detect widespread perceptions (regardless of the stories' literal truth);[59] it may help us also to understand the relationship between different sources, that author x's account is engaging more with the account of author y than it is with the historical reality of Achaemenid Persia. Collating the sources and presenting them in silent juxtaposition may also, in many cases, be the only strategy available to us in reconstructing a particular feature of social practice or court ceremonial, and the evidence may – in so far as it converges – have, or appear to have, a cumulative weight. Such an approach is also fraught with danger, however. We run the risk, first, of subjecting stories to a literal interpretation which they cannot bear. Herodotus' account of the conspiracy of the Seven against the false Smerdis, for example, and of the difficulty they faced in gaining access to the pretender, 'seems to indicate', according to Briant, that 'at the time of the first kings, all of the aristocrats were subject to the usual rules of royal protocol that were meant to control access to the interior of the palace'; this leads him then to interrogate the possible sources for the inaccessibility of the later kings.[60] As we shall see, moreover, in discussion of Persian royal women (see below, Chapter 3), an eagerness to distil the various strands of disparate evidence into a firm protocol may elide the very different functions of Greek stories *in their contexts*.

In short, the use of Greek sources for the writing of Persian history requires more than the mechanical excision of an author's bias, more than the briefest characterisation of their ideological position vis-à-vis 'Oriental despotism'. Just as it is important to know the Achaemenid world from the inside,[61] Greek representations, Greek engagements with Near Eastern tradition require more than a cursory detour. They cannot neatly be classified as either 'factual' or tabloid invention.[62] There are, however, other aspects to the recent reconstruction of the narrative of Persian history which in many ways are independent of a close reading of the sources. Many of the main changes in direction in Persian history have been decided as much on the grounds of inherent plausibility as on the basis of close argument from evidence. It is to this pattern that we now turn.

2

The Persian Version

Truth-loving Persians do not dwell upon
The trivial skirmish fought near Marathon ...
    Robert Graves, 'The Persian version' (1948: 210)

'Hecataeus of Miletus speaks thus. I write these things as seems to me to be true; for the accounts of the Greeks are many and, as it appears to me, absurd.' So Herodotus' early fifth-century predecessor began his work. When Hecataeus, or other early Greek logographers, were faced by a mythological account which was hard to square with everyday experience (the tradition, for example, that the entrance to the Underworld was guarded by the dog Cerberus) they breezily rationalised it – though to modern readers' eyes the revised version may seem scarcely less fantastical.[1] The historian of Persia is often found in a similar position. The writing of Persian history often depends on an act of imagination, the mental effort required to try to envisage things from the Persian point of view rather than through the prism of the Persians' adversaries.[2]

A very clear example of where this change in orientation has made a striking difference is in the story of Persian art. To previous generations, or at least to some,[3] the term Persian art

– except perhaps in so far as it meant art that was made in Persia – would have appeared an oxymoron. (Similar positions have been taken concerning Roman art. It was under the influence of Sir John Beazley that, in the classification system of the Ashmolean Library at Oxford, Roman art was included as a subheading of the History of Technology, on the grounds that it consisted of Roman copies of Greek originals.[4]) How to classify the material that looked like Persian art then, not least the sculptured reliefs of Persepolis? How did it fit into the 'jigsaw puzzle of world art ... between Egyptian, Assyrian and Greek sculpture'?[5]

The answer was that it was the art of the Persians' subject peoples, and above all of the Greeks. Apparent support for this position was discovered in the so-called Susa Foundation Charter, unearthed in 1929, in which Darius portentously lists not only the goods from all corners of the earth that contributed to his palace at Susa – gold from Sardis and Bactria, lapis lazuli and cornelian from Sogdiana, turquoise from Chorasmia, and so on – but also the craftsmen who came together to create his 'great work':[6]

> The stone-cutters who worked the stone, those were Ionians and Sardians. The goldsmiths who worked the gold, those were Medes and Egyptians. The men who worked the wood, those were Sardians and Egyptians. The men who worked the baked brick, those were Babylonians. The men who adorned the wall, those were Medes and Egyptians.

The hunt was then on for Greek features in the masonry of

Persepolis and other sites, and evidence was swiftly found in the hair and drapery of the reliefs. Even named Greeks were put forward as responsible for Achaemenid art, with Telephanes from the Ionian city of Phocaea (whose connection with Persia is attested only by Pliny several hundred years later) being termed the 'grand master of the Persepolis friezes'.[7] In the most extreme formulation of this narrative of Persian art, in a series of lectures on 'Archaic Greek art against its historical background', Gisela Richter indeed lists Persia as one of a series of 'artistic dependencies of Greece in Asia'.[8] The relationship between Greeks and Persians was a reciprocal one for Richter, but a distinctly unequal exchange: whereas the Greeks saved Persian art from what would otherwise have been its 'uniformly Oriental character', the Persians gave unemployed Greek artists 'opportunities'.[9] Any perceived faults in the sculptures of Persepolis, moreover, are seen as the result of Greek artists' subordination to restrictive 'Oriental conceptions'.[10]

Beginning with the Swedish scholar Carl Nylander, however, and his *Ionians in Pasargadae*, and with Margaret Cool Root's monograph on *The King and Kingship* as a later landmark, this position has been progressively revised. The influence of Ionian craftsmen has by no means been eliminated: it can be seen, for example, in the masonry techniques used in the building of Cyrus' tomb at Pasargadae.[11] But the combination of Greek models with others is seen – far from constituting an 'originality of incompetence', in the dreadful phrase of Bernard Berenson[12] – to be part of a conscious design. Ionians, Babylonians and others worked in teams. The tidy allocation of tasks to peoples in the Susa Foundation

2. The Persian Version

Charter, however, is not so much a workplan as an ideological statement of the reach of the King's power. In combining styles and techniques drawn from different peoples – Greek masonry techniques with a stepped platform drawing on Elamite or Anatolian traditions, to pursue the example of Cyrus' tomb – Persian art embodied the Persians' claim to have subsumed previous empires, providing a neat parallel to the Kings' accumulation of royal titles or listing of subject peoples (see Fig. 6).[13] And even the style of masonry of the vast platform on which Persepolis was built – 'massive irregular stones, perfectly bonded without mortar' – has been interpreted as an expression of Darius' similar bonding of the disparate parts of his empire (see Fig. 7).[14] 'Borrowing then', in the words of Heleen Sancisi-Weerdenburg, 'is borrowing of elements and details, which in the newly formed syntax of Achaemenid art acquire a significance which is different from previous usage of the same motifs'.[15] And the seamless uniformity of style from king to king[16] – a uniformity both in sculptural motifs and in the motifs of royal inscriptions – should not be interpreted as slavish emulation of royal predecessors but as a deliberate, even artful,[17] statement of the timeless nature of Persian power.

A similar change in approach (again one in which Root's contribution has been pivotal) has taken place with regard to the *interaction* of Achaemenid and other influences in the art of the empire's fringes. Rather than seeing Persian features as somehow passive and residual – clinging on, as Hellenism went on its long march – by the slightest 'rhetorical redirection'[18] the picture is transformed into one in which Achaemenid design actively influenced the art of the Persian

Fig. 6. Pasargadae: the tomb of Cyrus.

empire's western margins. The resulting culture of any region is not the outcome of some straightforward grafting on of external influences, but represents a genuine symbiosis, something new and dynamic.[19] And the more the archaeological

Fig. 7. Persepolis: detail of the platform on which the complex of palaces was constructed.

record is expanded, the greater the likelihood that further evidence will be uncovered of the impact of Achaemenid models.[20]

These changes may seem relatively unproblematic. Though tying any 'art' to an ethnic identity is questionable – and Greek art is no more easily definable arguably than Persian – the notion that one culture could be defined solely or primarily in terms of its peripheral relationship to another seems outmoded. We can look back now and see how such a conclusion may have seemed natural in the context of the attempt to make sense of an emerging set of Near Eastern 'arts',[21] but we do so from the vantage point of a different paradigm, one in which (in general) we do not seek to establish a pecking order of world cultures.[22]

Other aspects of the rhetorical redirection of Persian history may be similarly uncontroversial. The notion (as we will see, not always expressed so clearly) that the Persian empire was languishing in decadence for the 150 years after the Persian wars, merely waiting for Alexander to deliver the fatal blow, is so inherently flimsy (or so it seems now), that only the slightest counter-argument (if so, how could it have held on for so long?[23]) should at least unsettle any such view; the Persepolis tablets then provide cumulative evidence of the depth of the control – or at least of the administrative infra-structure[24] – of Persian administration. (Though it is right to challenge the assumption of Persian decadence,[25] we should not replace it with an assumption of Persian resilience.) For Cambyses to be grouped with his father Cyrus as one of the 'builders of the empire',[26] though it may cause an initial surprise given his common reputation, is merited simply on the basis of his extension of the empire to Egypt, regardless of Herodotus' account of his subsequent overreaching. Likewise, few would probably dispute that the wars fought between the Persians and the Greeks loom larger in our sources than they merit in terms of their significance to the empire as a whole. Recent scholars might sometimes seem to be shrinking the Persian wars almost to the point of perversity as a kind of *jeu d'esprit* – questioning whether these 'skirmishes at the far western frontier' had *any* effect on the 'daily business of government', or referring passingly and simply to Thermopylae as an 'utter defeat' of the Greeks, as if such a silent revision of a long tradition might somehow slip by unnoticed[27] – but some such reduction in scale provides a useful reminder that the King *must* also have been concerned with other frontiers and provinces, even if we only glimpse them in the surviving evidence.

Another common pattern in recent accounts is the ascription of sound strategic motives for actions, independently of the sources. So, to extend the example of Cambyses' invasion of Egypt, how are we to explain his campaign in the first place? 'Evidently', in the words of one recent history, 'Cambyses decided that the western frontier of his territory needed to be stabilized and, perhaps, that Egypt could be advantageously annexed by war or diplomacy'.[28] According to Briant likewise, the invasion was all for sensible strategic reasons, the inevitable consequence of the shared ambition of Egyptians and Persians for control of the Levant.[29] All of this is anodyne and largely unobjectionable. It is likely perhaps that any king would have thought to 'stabilise' his control of his kingdom, whether or not he was capable of formulating this in sound, strategic language. The desire to annexe Egypt is a reasonable extrapolation, perhaps, simply from the fact of its having been annexed. And the thesis of tension over control of the Levant is confirmed by a long pattern of similar conflict over that territory, not least the series of Syrian wars fought between Alexander's successor kingdoms, the Seleucids and the Ptolemies.

Nevertheless, it is important to be clear as to what of this reconstruction is rooted in the ancient sources, and what is not. What evidence do we have for motives? On the one hand, the Persian royal inscriptions give ample evidence of royal satisfaction at conquest for conquest's sake. In the words inscribed on the freestanding statue of Darius at Susa (a statue later used for target practice by Alexander's troops[30]), the King ordered it to be made in Egypt so that 'whoever will see it in time to come will know that a Persian man holds Egypt'.[31] This and similar material from the Persian context might arguably offer some kind of frame, a set of margins, for the imaginative extrapolation of the King's motives. On the other hand, Herodotus ascribes the invasion of Egypt to a choice of personal grudges arising from a Perso-Egyptian marriage alliance: according to one version, Amasis had passed off his usurped predecessor's daughter as his own; according to another, the marriage was to Cyrus rather than Cambyses, but the Egyptian girl soon eclipsed Cyrus' wife Cassandane in the King's affections, and the boy Cambyses promised to turn Egypt upside down when he was older, to avenge his mother; in yet a further twist, the Egyptians (Herodotus reports) make the claim that Nitetis was in fact Cambyses' mother, so in some sense appropriating their invader.[32] Interpreting this material is by no means fruitless – though the task is complicated by the multiple contexts from which it, most likely, originated: Egyptian, Greek and Persian.[33] (And Persian kings, like other monarchs across history, may well have been informed on occasion by personal grudges.[34]) Anything further, however – anything, that is, which is not rooted in any of the relevant source material, or in reasoned analogy from other periods – is essentially speculative, and should be recognised as such.[35] Other such reconstructions, moreover, are arguably more tendentious: Xerxes' withdrawal from Greece, presented in the Greek sources as a harum-scarum flight, has been argued more recently to have been a 'strategic decision not to employ the navy in another battle, since the Phoenician ships had proved to be unsuitable for naval manoeuvre in Greek waters'.[36] How far any withdrawal is planned or forced is perhaps never clear, always subject to differing judgements; there is no reason to assent unquestioningly to either extreme interpretation. There is equally, however, a danger that we eliminate every mischance, every blemish of failure from our account of the ups and downs of the Persian empire.

One final pattern that needs to be addressed is a kind of 'rhetorical redirection' applied to Greek narratives, whereby the perspective of those narratives is silently amended. One example is the treatment of a critical episode in the Ionian revolt against Persian rule, the moment at which the Athenians (who had answered the appeal for help made by Aristagoras of Miletus) burnt the temple of Cybebe at Sardis. The Athenians' participation in the revolt is portrayed by Herodotus as a fateful decision: the twenty ships which they contributed are described in a Homeric phrase as 'the beginning of evils for Greeks and barbarians'.[37] Their burning of the temple was subsequently latched onto by Darius – Herodotus' Darius, that is – as a justification for revenge, and in the Herodotean account the King instructed his servant to remind him as he took his meal by repeating three times the mantra 'oh master, remember the Athenians'. The burning of the temple itself is very clearly presented as an accident, however:[38]

Most of the houses there were made out of reeds, and even the ones which were made out of bricks had roofs thatched with reeds. Consequently, as soon as one of the houses had been set alight by a soldier, the fire spread from house to house and engulfed the whole city … During the conflagration of Sardis a sanctuary of the local goddess Cybebe was burnt down, and later the Persians made this their excuse for the retaliatory burning of sanctuaries they did in Greece.

It is easy to be cynical about this account of accidental sacrilege. One prominent historian of Greek religion, Robert Parker, wryly noted in 1983 that Greeks only ever burn temples by accident (while foreigners always do it on purpose).[39] By contrast, however, one account of the episode by a historian of Persia makes this step for us. The Persians' quashing of the revolt was 'not a simple victorious progress', Amélie Kuhrt writes. 'The rebels even succeeded in burning the stronghold of Sardis.'[40] Likewise another recent account describes how 'the initial impetus led to a partially successful assault on Sardis, the regional capital defended by the satrap and his Lydian allies (the outskirts were charred, but the citadel was not taken)'.[41] Herodotus' account of the Ionian revolt is scathing of the Ionians (and many have interpreted his description of the Athenians' ships as a pejorative comment on their participation[42]): far from being presented as noble freedom fighters, they are a fractious and in many cases lazy group, whose leaders (with the exception of one, Dionysius of Phocaea) are self-serving.[43] Both these modern accounts, by contrast, are 'focalised' through Persian eyes. Perhaps the claim of accidental damage is so transparently foolish that it can justifiably be elided (within the context of a very spare and concise narrative),[44] but these recent narratives ascribe (implicitly, at least) straightforward motives to the Greek rebels, giving them credit for putting up a surprisingly good fight or for partial success, and all on the basis of a Greek narrative with a very different perspective. No matter that we might agree with the historical conclusions reached, the fact that they are reached silently in this way, that the complex texture of the Herodotean narrative is essentially airbrushed, should make us uneasy.

Similar adaptations are made to the narrative of the subsequent Persian wars. So, for example, Kuhrt's account of the aftermath of Plataea, in which the Athenians and their allies mopped up certain Persian positions in Europe, is again presented from the perspective of a Persian rearguard: 'despite heroic resistance offered by several local Persian commanders, most Achaemenid strategic positions were lost'.[45] Jack Balcer likewise identifies so entirely with a Persian perspective, even as he exploits Herodotus' account of the war, as to make passing comment on 'the petty parochialism and antagonisms' of the Greek world, the 'few Athenian zealots [who] tried unsuccessfully to defend the Acropolis' from its Persian assailants, or Mardonius' 'loyal Theban forces'.[46] Balcer has indeed taken this approach further in attempting to tell the story of the Persian wars against Greece from the Persian point of view.[47] The problem is that this is to a very large extent impossible, as for the narrative of the Persian wars we are (but for a very few shafts of light from other sources) utterly dependent on Greek sources. We may guess at sound, strategic reasons for why Persians did things, or even imagine a 'long-term Aegean policy [of] extending a measure of control to European Greece',[48] and it is perhaps necessary that we should perform this kind of mental exercise as a control on the Greek sources. We should not imagine, however, that these are anything other than imaginative reconstructions. Thucydides famously said of the speeches that he introduced into his *History* that he made his speakers say what it was appropriate for them to say in the context;[49] we should be wary of supplying motives for the Persians in similar fashion.

There is also a danger inherent in this approach of under-estimating those sources that we do have. This emerges clearly from the competing modern accounts of the Persian wars. So, for example, according to Balcer, Thucydides was right in ascribing Greek victory to the mistakes of the Persians.[50] This is implicitly contrasted with the interpretation of Thucydides' predecessor, Herodotus, but also with 'the ancient idea of the victory of Athenian democracy over the indomitable forces of the enslaving oriental despotism of Achaemenid Persia'.[51] The latter position is scarcely ever formulated in such stark terms, and certainly not by Herodotus (who very often undercuts what appear at face value to be patriotic statements).[52] Thucydides' verdict, on the other hand, could almost be a summary of the account of the Persian wars given by Herodotus. Herodotus' account is indeed much more textured than it is generally credited with being and reflects a complex knowledge of Persian imperial ideology. To take just one example, in one of the inscriptions on his tomb at Naqsh-i-Rustam, Darius declares that he will not punish lightly on the basis of another man's report: in Roland Kent's translation, 'What a man says against a man, that does not convince me, until he satisfies the ordinance of good regulations.'[53] This is a theme which is not only reflected but which finds regular development in the *Histories*: in Darius' lengthy justification of the value of deceit (confounding the Persians' reputation for truth-telling), and in an elaborate discourse concerning slander within the Persian court.[54] Artabanus opines at length on the wickedness of slander, and the King himself punishes the Phoenicians at Salamis for denigrating the Ionians in the King's service, 'so that they who were base not slander men more noble', and yet slander and distrust are so rife in the King's court as to suggest the conclusion that they are an inevitable function of a monarchic system.[55] Clearly this is a moral which is very different from that of Darius at Naqsh-i-Rustam. However, as with other aspects of Herodotus' portrayal of the Persians – the imperative of imperial conquest, or the ideology of the King's rewarding his friends and exacting revenge on his enemies – his account is not so much a free composition as an intelligent rhapsody on themes which can be traced back to the King's own inscribed words.

Finding an easy place for the campaigns of Alexander within the narrative of Persian history is, by contrast to the Persian wars, a more challenging task. At one level, recent scholarship has precisely foregrounded the Achaemenid continuities in Alexander's rule, presenting him indeed as the 'last of the Achaemenids'. As Briant has observed, 'like any formula, this one has its limits and gives rise to contradictions of its own'.[56] One ironic (classicist's) response to the tag of 'last of the Achaemenids' has been to suggest that (like the Egyptians' attribution of an Egyptian mother to Cambyses) it is a form of appropriation on the part of Achaemenid historians: 'the empire was not strong enough to defeat Alexander even when his army was massively outnumbered, but did it then absorb him, the 'last' in its very long *durée*?'[57] At the same time, there is also a sense in which Persian historians have a surprising stake in a heroic narrative of Alexander. If the Persian empire had really been on its knees from the period of the Persian wars, a common turn of argument has it, it would not have taken a mighty conqueror to overwhelm it; conversely, the more resilient, the more well-founded the Persian empire is revealed to be, the greater is Alexander's achievement in casting it down. '[Alexander's conquest] was a remarkable achievement', in the words of Amélie Kuhrt, 'and the difficulties Alexander encountered in twelve years of continuous fighting bear witness to the remarkable solidity of the Achaemenid realm'.[58] According to Maria Brosius, similarly, the presentation of Darius III (Alexander's adversary) as weak and feeble 'provides a paradox ..., as a fight against a truly weak king would also diminish the extent of Alexander's victory'.[59] Greek historians, the line goes in essence, cannot have it both ways: they cannot make a claim for a neutered Persian empire and keep their conquering hero intact.[60] The Persian empire, conversely, can be portrayed as the victim of its own success (so implicitly reclaiming some of Alexander's victory): it was precisely because the empire 'had not been faced with any external threat' before that the Macedonian invasion could be successful.[61]

At another level, however, as the perpetrator of the destruction of Persepolis, Alexander is necessarily a villain. Accounts of Alexander by Persian historians place a greater emphasis on the violence of his campaigns than those of many, at least, of the Greek historians of the period.[62] So, for example, a recent history of Persia reveals a distinct flash of animus as it describes the reaction of the Egyptians waiting in the path of Alexander's army ('no doubt aghast at such total destruction and merciless punishment for neutrality as well as resistance'[63]) or talks in passing of the *violent* charge of Alexander's central cavalry' – as if it might have been pacific.[64] Alexander was 'merely a conqueror' in the words of another recent account, as confirmed by his 'short-term strategies, his military aggression, his violent reactions against any demonstration of resistance, the ruthless killing of local populations, and the destruction of cities and towns throughout this twelve-year campaign'.[65] Alexander has been condemned likewise for his ignorance of Persian customs, his failure to understand the ideology of kingship, or his 'skewed appropriation of Persian practice',[66] and – perhaps most strikingly of all – for the lack of 'sincerity' with which he 'tried to present himself as a legitimate king of Persia'.[67]

The point here is not that Alexander's violence (or political cynicism) should be airbrushed out, or that one should subscribe to a lazily heroising narrative, but only that one should take a reasonably dispassionate view of the violence perpetrated by both Greeks and Persians. Many of these judgements of Alexander are openly hostile. But, as Briant puts it starkly in the context of Darius' suppression of revolts, 'there is little doubt that the Persians resorted to the use of terror'. As he adds, Darius boasts of the massacre of 'every survivor of the Babylonian armies that he attacked on the banks of the Tigris and the Euphrates'.[68] For better or for worse, the evidence that Alexander delayed before putting Persepolis to the torch indicates that it was not the act of a *wanton* vandal (much as we may see it as such in retrospect), or the result of high jinks that got out of control (as one Greek version has it), but a deliberate action: designed perhaps to be seen to fulfil his claim of delivering vengeance for the Persian wars, or a sign of his failure to accommodate the local Persian nobility.[69] As for Alexander's misunderstandings and skewing of Persian practice, by the 'slightest rhetorical redirection' they could be portrayed very differently: as homages to Persian practice. They were clearly intended to appease the Persian nobility, and clearly also caused grave offence to many of his Greco-Macedonian followers. In the context of the kind of ideological tightrope that Alexander needed to walk in the light of his conquest – the need to fulfil the ideological promise of his campaign, while stepping into a new role in seeking to maintain his new power – can we reasonably expect more?[70] As Michel Austin has expressed it in a different context, 'the sincerity or otherwise' of Alexander's positions 'is perhaps not a relevant issue'.[71]

There is perhaps an interesting comparison to be made between the scholarly response to Alexander's accommodation with the Persians and Babylonians and Cambyses' with the Egyptians (discussed further in Chapter 4 below).[72] The issue of Cambyses' sincerity, for example, is never raised; occupying Persians are rightly assessed (as Alexander should be) as pragmatists. Recent scholars of Achaemenid history, on the other hand, have tended to characterise any collaborators with Alexander's rule as 'hostages' or as essentially reluctant.[73] In practice, however, in both cases both conqueror and conquered had strong practical motives for finding some accommodation. One scholar's 'educated guess', by contrast, of what the Babylonians would have made of Alexander is much more ambivalent: the 'change of dynasty will not have bothered them very much, if it could take place without bloodshed' – though 'it must have been very awkward to have a beardless king'.[74] Though we may hazard a guess at the comparative tally of casualties of war in either case (and doubtless Alexander's campaigns would emerge the bloodier), it is hard to escape the conclusion that the primary distinguishing factor here is our identification (or otherwise) with the Persians and their empire.

In writing of some heroising modern accounts of Alexander, Brian Bosworth has noted the irony that though 'Imperialism is no longer in fashion, [and] nor is aggression for its own sake ... a positively rose-tinted aura surrounds Alexander, the leader of one of the most successful wars of imperial aggrandizement, pursued wholly for gain and glory under the specious pretext of revenge'.[75] In the rush to correct Hellenocentric and unduly pejorative assessments of Persia, there are arguably similar dangers: that in the eagerness to prove that Persian imperialism had an impact, or that bad king Cambyses made successful additions to the empire, imperial expansion is presented by default as an unquestioned good; that the positive reactions of subject peoples are taken for granted in our narratives; and that Hellenocentrism gives way to an Iranocentrism.[76] Whether or not we should be seeking to assess ancient empires according to a kind of moral balance-sheet – judging whether the benefits they brought their subjects outweigh the violence perpetrated – is an open question. It is arguable that this model, derived from early twentieth-century debates on the pros and cons of modern imperialisms, under-estimates the complexity of the reactions of subject peoples.[77] Unquestionably, however, some focus on the impact of empire – for good or ill – is preferable to an assumed identification.

3

Family Fortunes

Failure of the European adventure opened the way to
harem intrigues, with all their deadly consequences.

A.T. Olmstead (1948: 266-7)

We turn now from the moral dimension of the empire as a
whole to the behaviour of kings and queens.

The close of Herodotus' account of the Persian wars envis-
ages the Persian empire as in disarray.[1] While his army stays
behind to suffer further ignominious defeats, Xerxes slinks
back to his court at Susa, indulging en route in an extraordinarily complex love intrigue. Echoing the story of Candaules
(who fell in love with his own wife) at the opening of the
Histories,[2] Xerxes falls in love with the wife of his brother,
Masistes. Since he cannot fulfil his desire more straightforwardly, the King takes a more circuitous approach, marrying
his son to the daughter of Masistes, Artaynte. On returning to
Susa, however, he then falls in love with Artaynte herself.
Visiting her one day, wearing a magnificent robe woven by his
wife, queen Amestris, he tells Artaynte that she can ask for any
present that she wishes. She asks for the robe, and – despite
Xerxes asking her to think again – persists in her request.
When she wears the robe at court, Amestris is furious and

plots her revenge. At the King's birthday banquet, an occasion on which he is obliged to honour any request,[3] Amestris asks her husband for Masistes' wife. Masistes duly returns home to find his wife mutilated – her breasts, nose, ears, lips and tongue cut off and fed to the dogs.

The very final chapters of the *Histories* which follow – through their account of the crucifixion of a prominent Persian at the border of Europe and Asia, the Hellespont (on the order of the father of the later Athenian leader Pericles), and through a closing anecdote taking the reader back to the origins of the Persian empire under Cyrus – all suggest that the mantle of empire has passed from Persia to Athens, that a historical cycle has been completed. 'Soft lands breed soft men', Cyrus advises his fellow Persians in almost the final words; 'it is impossible for one and the same country to produce remarkable crops and good fighting men'.[4] The clear implication is that the Persians have been corrupted by the soft lands that they had conquered – and that the degeneracy of Xerxes' court and his defeat in Greece are all symptoms of this decline.

This passage is central to the version of the Persian empire as lying prone from the time of the Persian wars to the expedition of Alexander. In the same vein, Herodotus' dramatisation of the Persian debate on the wisdom of their expedition to Greece shows Xerxes argue (in terms again that reveal Herodotus' knowing engagement with the genealogising style of Persian royal pronouncements) that the failure to attack Greece will leave them open to attack themselves:[5]

If I fail to punish the Athenians, may I no longer be descended from Darius, the son of Hystaspes, son of

3. Family Fortunes

Arsames, son of Teispes, son of Achaemenes. I am sure the Athenians will do something if we do not; to judge by their past moves, they will certainly make a move against our country, since these are the people who burnt down Sardis and invaded Asia. It is impossible for either side to withdraw now; the only question is whether or not we actively take the initiative. And in the end either all Persia will be in Greek hands, or all Greece will be in Persian hands; there is no middle ground in this war.

The Persian wars were thus implicitly a battle for survival for Persia as much as Greece. As discussed above (Chapter 2), the thesis – if we can even call it that – that Persia merely hobbled through the century and a half from the Persian wars to the Macedonian invasion is one which (now at least) seems hard to sustain. It is equally hard to understand how Herodotus could seriously have maintained that Persia had imploded in the light of Greek victory – writing, as many believe now, under the shadow of the Peloponnesian war in which the Persians were decisive off-stage figures.[6] (It is possible, indeed, that Xerxes' presentation of war against Greece as a battle for survival is to be read – like Mardonius' characterisation of Greece as pre-eminently fertile[7] – as delusional, as the symptom of a kind of imperial paranoia.) It becomes necessary, at very least, to soften the effect of his final chapters: to suppose that his prolepsis indicates a decisive pendulum swing, that the Persian empire will henceforth be the victim of Greek aggression rather than vice versa, but not that Persia has somehow evaporated from history.[8]

This implicit historical judgement, together with the association of military decline and moral decadence which Herodotus' conclusion establishes, has, unsurprisingly, excited strong reactions[9] from the new Achaemenid historians. In particular, scholars have co-opted the emphasis in much scholarship of the last thirty years on the Greek-barbarian polarity in Greek thought, and on the western construction of the 'Orient' more generally, to suggest that such characterisations of Persia are driven by the inversion of *Greek* norms. This reaction is well summarised by Amélie Kuhrt:[10]

> All the Greek writers were fascinated by the wealth and power of the Persian rulers, so they often recount stories of court intrigue and the moral decadence that comes from indulging in unlimited luxury. In such anecdotes, the Persian king appears as an essentially weak figure, a prey to the machinations of powerful women and sinister eunuchs. This is an inversion of Greek social and political norms, with which we, as Europeans have usually identified: the image of the cowardly, effeminate Persian monarch has exercised a strong influence through the centuries, making the Persian empire into a powerful 'other' in European Orientalism, contrasted with 'western' bravery and masculinity ... We must remember this in studying the Persian empire: the popular and widespread impression of its political system is fundamentally flawed ...

More recently, stories of the excesses of the Persian court have been interpreted in new ways. In a number of cases, what are presented, or appear as, excessive or barbaric acts in the

3. Family Fortunes

Greek sources can be explained, in a Near Eastern context, as actions whose symbolism has been (wilfully or unintentionally) misunderstood. (This form of interpretation of Greek accounts of Persian history long predates, in fact, the new Achaemenid historiography.) So, for example, the notorious episode in which Xerxes whips the water of the Hellespont as a punishment for its destruction of the Persians' pontoon bridge should be seen, not as a sign of the King's hybristic excess, but as an expression of his Zoroastrian beliefs.[11] Xerxes' marching his expeditionary force through the bisected body of the son of the Lydian Pythius – who had rashly asked that his son be spared participating in the campaign – may have its explanation in a long pattern of Near Eastern purification rites.[12] Similarly, the story of sexual intrigue with which Herodotus ends his portrayal of the Persian court can be revealed to be shot through with folkloric motifs.[13] The gift of a robe around which the story revolves may be a symbol of royal sovereignty. The name Masistes given to Xerxes' brother can be connected to an Old Persian word Mathishta – highest or greatest, possibly a title. The suggestion, then, is that the story is a kind of allegorical version of the rivalry between the brothers, misunderstood by Herodotus: that 'under the surface of this romantic tale might be hidden an attempt to rebel by a brother of the king'.[14]

A similar approach has been taken to stories of the Persians' alleged culinary excesses. Xenophon, in his eulogy of the Spartan Agesilaus, characterises the Persian court as in a constant search for new delicacies to titillate the King's jaded palate; the final section of his *Cyropaedia* sees the Persians eating and drinking so excessively from dawn to dusk that they need to be carried from their banquets.[15] This, however, misses the ideological dimension of the Persian banquet, and the vast numbers of those to be fed: these highly staged affairs provided an opportunity for the expression of the tributary relationship of subject peoples, and for the reward of loyalty. Some of this was recognised, in fact, by both Herodotus and the fourth-century Heracleides of Cyme: though the Persians roasted whole oxen, horses, camels or donkeys in giant ovens, their meals consisted (in Herodotus' account) of lots of small courses; Heracleides portrays the Persian banquet as relatively frugal, with leftovers being taken away in helpfully provided bags, or being given to the guards.[16]

In addition to these kinds of explanations in terms of Near Eastern context, other violent actions can be explained in terms of sound motives of *Realpolitik*. So, for example, the passing mention, in Herodotus' account of Cambyses' spell of madness in Egypt, of the King's having arrested twelve aristocratic Persians (on a trifling charge) and burying them alive head downwards, can be seen in the context of Cambyses' establishing his authority among the Persian elite: 'If we reject the "moralizing" explanation of the behaviour of Cambyses ("cruelty," "madness"), we may surmise that he was actually taking reprisals against the great families that had expressed opposition to some of his decrees.'[17] That burying alive was practised as a punishment is not impossible (this is not a solitary example in our sources[18]); once the moral colouring is removed from the anecdote, however, it is revealed apparently as an instance of royal pragmatism.[19]

Other instances of violent excess can simply be dismissed, rather than rationalised, on the grounds that they are the product of Greek fantasies. Emblematic here – and emblematic also of the condescending Western attitude to the Orient from which Persian history needs to be liberated, according to Sancisi-Weerdenburg[20] – is the case of Persian royal women. If Persian kings are frequently cruel and violent in the Greek sources, then their queens appear arguably even crueller. The punishment exacted on the wife of Masistes by Amestris – her mutilation and the feeding of her body parts to the dogs – is but one example of a long pattern across Greek accounts of the fifth and fourth centuries.[21] This kind of behaviour – together with their intercessions to avert the punishments of their family or favourites[22] – is seen as the reflection of the enormous power wielded by royal women: Xerxes' mother, Darius' wife, Atossa, was said by Herodotus to have held 'complete power' in the court, to the extent that she was pivotal in her son Xerxes' succession.[23] It is also perceived as a reflection of Persian women's masculinity. Atossa, we hear from a fifth-century source, Hellanicus of Lesbos,[24]

> concealed her female nature and was the first monarch to wear the tiara and trousers; she also established the service of eunuchs and the issuing of judgements in writing. She subdued many peoples and was extremely warlike and manly in all her accomplishments.

By contrast, their husbands and sons are effeminate: so, famously, as Xerxes, from on top of his viewing mound at Salamis, observed the seeming bravery of the Carian queen Artemisia, he observed that his men had become women and his women men.[25]

All this is seen very differently by recent historians of Persia. The pernicious role attributed to royal women should be seen not as historical fact but 'literary cliché'.[26] Such stories are a function of Greek misogyny, or of Greek ignorance.[27] They should be dismissed as fiction. And yet they are nevertheless used as a basis for the reconstruction of what can appear a sanitised, 'apple-pie' picture of the role of Persian royal women. 'What is described as the brutal revenge of Persian queens', according to Maria Brosius, 'turns out to be the duty of a mother who has to use her position to undo injustice which has fallen on one of her family.'[28] 'The women's main responsibility was the welfare and security of the royal family.'[29] On the one hand, the Greek sources support the evidence of Persepolis texts – of prominent women travelling with their retinues – in suggesting the existence of 'positively active, enterprising and resolute' Persian women.[30] On the other hand, the lurid stories of Herodotus and Xenophon are distilled into a kind of constitutional framework for punishment in the Persian court which gives royal women a precise and bounded place:[31]

> The punishment of high-ranking Persian officials or members of the royal family ... was the duty of the king alone. He was informed about possible plots and rebellions, and any signs of disloyalty from any of his subjects who exceeded the limit of their position. The suspects were always taken before the King, whose sentence was the only valid verdict. Women could not interfere with this verdict, but with the consent of the King they could alter the form of punishment. Within a rather restricted

range women could punish some individuals directly; but they could do so only by taking advantage of a situation in which the King was obliged to grant a request.

Perhaps the first question to address in response is whether you can reasonably square the different positions maintained here. Can we credit Persian queens for being both enterprising and public, on the one hand, and concerned primarily with their families, on the other? To caricature the end point of the argument, Persian women were enterprising and full of initiative (unlike their Greek counterparts); but they were not cruel or nasty; or, if they were, it was with good reason (family loyalty), or was anyway approved by their male relatives. It is hard to suppress the suspicion that the approach to the sources evidenced here is one driven primarily by the desire to undo negative perceptions of Persian women.

In particular, the defence of Persian women (never, of course, explicitly formulated as a defence) that their punishments of others were motivated by a mother's duty crucially misses the Greek ideological context for such stories.[32] These Persian women are not alone (in the Greeks' eyes) in their cool cruelty or in their desire to protect the interests of their families. Herodotus' *Histories* alone includes countless parallels from a range of cultures: the Egyptian queen Nitocris, who avenged her brother's death by drowning all his enemies in an underground chamber; the wife of Sesostris, who – trapped with her family in a burning house – devised the plan by which they escaped, commanding two of her sons to lie down in the flames as a bridge for the others; or, perhaps most graphically of all, the Cyrenean ruler Pheretime, who punished the people of Barca for the death of her son, by cutting off the breasts of the Barcaean women and using them to stud the city walls, before impaling their husbands.[33]

Persian women also play a central role, across a range of authors, in the initiation of wars.[34] Even though Herodotus' Persians thought it ridiculous to start a war because of the abduction of a woman,[35] a number of different versions explain Cambyses' invasion of Egypt in exactly those terms.[36] It is, likewise, Darius' wife Atossa in Herodotus' account who first implants the idea of invading Greece into her husband's mind: she goes to Darius in bed and pleads with him to show that he is a real man by annexing Greece.[37] Her ostensible motive is that she wants Greek servant girls to attend her, her real reason to fulfil a promise made to her Greek doctor Democedes, desperate to return to his homeland of Croton. Like the story preserved in one fragmentary Greek historian of the King ordering the invasion of Greece because of his love of Attic figs,[38] the story of Atossa's approach – with its implicit conflation of Darius' sexual and military prowess – forms part of a tradition that serves to belittle Persian motives. It also, however, has a more serious message. In monarchies, the moral of these stories might be said to go, the personal *is* political; to use personal motives loosely then as an implicit *justification* for violent actions simply misses the point.

So the Greeks had a reason to latch on to stories of Persian queens' cruelty – in so far as it fed the moral that this was what happened in societies where women were given undue (to the Greeks) political influence. Bluntly, however, might these stories be true? It would clearly be wrong to revert to the assumption that the Greek characterisations of Persian women are simply and necessarily accurate; on the other hand, it would be wrong to dismiss these anecdotes too glibly as without any foundation. As another historian of the Persian relationship with the Greek world, David Lewis, once observed (with characteristic cynicism), in the light of modern horrors – contemporary readers can substitute their own examples – it is hard to disbelieve stories of cruelty:[39]

> I am myself disposed to take seriously stories of the irrational caprice and wanton cruelty of monarchs. Nothing is reported of Periander, tyrant of Corinth, which does not find ready parallels in well-attested information about Ali Pasha of Iannina at the beginning of the nineteenth century, and, allowing for some differences of institutions, the Persian court will be subject to the same kind of pressures and insecurities which have afflicted the courts of absolute monarchs down to the time of Stalin and perhaps beyond.

Impalement and mutilation are the regular ends of the liar kings (the rebels against Darius' throne) of the Behistun inscription – and indeed standard punishments for the Assyrians before. 'It was customary', as Pierre Briant puts it.[40] And a recent history of Iran has traced similar patterns of unaccountable royal violence across the ages, explaining it in terms of the lack of a sound legal footing for monarchic rule.[41]

Another possible response to the tradition of kings' and queens' cruelty is to accept its historicity but to refrain from a 'moralising' stance in regard to it. Whether this is a wise position is not straightforward, however. On the one hand, we might reasonably hold that the exercise of giving brownie points to one ancient culture or another for its superior moral position is an unsatisfactory one, bound to degenerate into reductive anachronism. (After all, it might be objected, it is the casual default moralising of previous generations of historians against which recent work has reacted.) On the other hand, to explain away the possibly frequent (if not systematic) use of torture, say, as simply the reflection of time-worn Near Eastern practice might also make one uneasy.[42] Passing over such unpalatable aspects – or, still worse, *wishing* them to be untrue – arguably betrays a no less reductive moralising perspective. It also takes away the opportunity to assess what such practices may tell us more broadly about the society in question. A recent work by an Old Testament scholar has made use of comparisons between Achaemenid torture – most graphically the technique of the 'hollowed-out trough' described in Plutarch's *Artoxerxes* – and recent American abuse of prisoners in Iraq. Bruce Lincoln writes of:[43]

a later moment in Achaemenian history … when the empire finds it increasingly difficult to contain the contradiction between its discourse and its practice. Having overcome the problem of moral hesitation by wrapping even its most distasteful actions in an ennobling, sanctifying discourse, the empire now faces the prospect of moral exhaustion, in which its animating discourse loses all credibility… In order to avoid that danger, it becomes necessary for the leaders and foot soldiers of the empire to repersuade themselves …

We do not have to find this compelling as a narrative, or to share some of the more negative views of Persian culture expressed by modern historians and critics,[44] to question what impact the use of extreme punishments had on the Persian elite, or how such practices should be understood alongside the lofty idealism of the royal inscriptions.

This awkward position that we find ourselves in, finally, is perhaps the inevitable result of the resolve of recent scholars to assess Persian history and society within its own terms, and in a Near Eastern context. To try to avoid seeing his or her subject in terms of default modern assumptions, the historian must, of course, first and foremost attempt this kind of sympathetic reconstruction. So long as it is a subsequent step, however, it is no less a part of the historian's role to stand back and assess a given society in as dispassionate terms as possible, even explicitly through a modern (and comparative) lens.[45]

Doing so might be healthy indeed in another respect. There is often, it seems, a lurking competitiveness between scholars of different fields – a competitiveness which surely runs the risk of distorting our understanding – which could usefully be drawn out. Not far, for example, below the surface of treatments of Persian women, lie claims about the relative lack of freedom of Greek women. Stories of the excess and violence of Persian queens reflect Greek misogyny, we are told – and so in a sense they do: Persian women are clearly serving as examples of how ('proper', i.e. Greek) women should not behave, but how they might behave if they too were subject to a monarchy.[46] But at the same time as Persian women's role is also carefully circumscribed (they cannot go beyond certain constitutional limits), a clear contrast is implied between

Greek women, essentially housebound, and Persians, gadding about in (closed[47]) carriages. *We* have 'enterprising and resolute women'![48] Maria Brosius tellingly highlights Herodotus' story of the wife of Intaphernes (one of Darius' fellow conspirators), who intercedes for her brother's life (in preference to her husband's) with the King, Darius:[49] 'it is ... remarkable that a woman takes an active role in the story, seeking an audience with the king in order to plead for her family'.[50] The story is taken as confirmation of a picture of Persian women's 'great concern for the defence and preservation of the family', and of the Persian woman's ability to use 'all possible means' if 'that structure became endangered'. Where other Greek stories of Persian women are dismissed as sensational in-fill,[51] this story (for no obvious reason) provides a solid foundation for a historical conclusion.

Both extreme visions here – the view of enterprising Persian women and of their suppressed Greek foils – need to be softened. The image of the Greek citizen wife, demurely weaving, with her face painted to exaggerate the extent to which she did not need to go outside the household, is an ideal type; vase images show us (lower-status) Greek women engaged in all forms of outdoor activity.[52] Conversely, in the Persian context, our evidence mostly concerns rare high-status women.[53] Achaemenid historians have been, perhaps understandably, leery of employing terms such as 'harem' (though acknowledging the possibility of 'women's quarters'), to distance themselves from stereotyped images of secluded women and their eunuch attendants.[54] But as analysis from other societies has increasingly shown, the harem does not exclude women's mobility or influence; likewise, eunuchs may play an important role (in harem, and court more generally) which is worthy of historical investigation.[55] Moreover, though Persian women feature in seal engravings – and though we might want to give weight to Herodotus' story of Darius commissioning a gold statue of his favourite wife, Artystone[56] – it remains a striking fact that in all the art of Persepolis, there is not a single image of a woman, and only one of a female animal[57] – apart, that is, from one piece of Greek statuary, perversely termed the 'greatest treasure' of Persepolis by Olmstead.[58] Evidence of the portrayal of women in other contexts may disprove any formal 'restriction' or ban on the representation of women,[59] but what is at issue is perhaps less stark: the meaning to be ascribed to a convention, even one limited to the sculptural art of Persepolis.

Any sense of overt or tacit competition over the position of women in Greece or Persia – like the identification of any single ancient author as having a more enlightened attitude to the position of women than his contemporaries – is quite simply absurd. (In this respect at least, we can count our own societies, with all their faults, preferable without looking for validation in antiquity.) A similar dispassionate lens is perhaps required in other contexts. We should not seek to minimise the violence endemic in the Greek world – Thucydides' unsparing narrative of the Peloponnesian war should provide a corrective if so. However, the marching of an army through the bisected remains of a human victim – or if we deem that unhistorical, the impalement of a vanquished rebel – is a violent, even shocking, act, no matter that it might have Hittite precedent. Likewise, in their accounts of the luxury of Persian 'haute cuisine', 'it is quite obvious', at one level, 'that the Greeks were not exaggerating'.[60] The descriptions of Heracleides and others of the exotic foodstuffs of the Persian banquet – of animals like gazelles roasted whole – are, in general terms, corroborated in the tablets of Persepolis.[61] Greek authors may have missed the political symbolism of the King's banquets, as they missed the symbolism of Xerxes' whipping of the Hellespont or of much else. They may also have moulded the material at their disposal into a narrative of Persian moral and sensory atrophy which suited their own position. But they were not merely inventing an image of Persian luxury *ex nihilo*.[62] A roasted gazelle is a roasted gazelle, after all.

4

Live and Let Live

In the dignified, respectful images of the nations and peoples of the realm we seem to see empire also from the peoples' point of view and we sense a notion almost of a commonwealth, an oecumenical brotherhood under the respected and beloved father figure of the Great King.

Carl Nylander (1979: 355)

We move now from the personal sphere to the broader canvas of the empire at large. What kind of empire did the Achaemenid Kings preside over? How positive was the role of the Kings towards the satrapies of their empire? And what attitude was evinced by the imperial subjects towards the Kings?

As in other areas of the history of Achaemenid Persia, there has been a significant shift in scholarly perceptions. Herodotus' accounts of the depradations of Cambyses in Egypt or of Xerxes in Babylon have been shown to be either grossly exaggerated or misunderstood. Other documentary evidence from Egypt, as we will see, reveals the Egyptians' accommodation with their new Persian rulers. And Herodotus' account has been shown (in a famous article by Amélie Kuhrt and Susan Sherwin-White) to have been misread as suggesting that Xerxes pillaged the cult statue of Bel-Marduk (an assumption

on which scholars then built), when it is evident from Herodotus' words that the statue was in fact another one located
within the sanctuary.[1] The Persian Kings' reputation, more
broadly, for tolerance of their subject peoples' religious cultures has never been unmixed – due, in large part, to Cyrus'
biblical image.[2] However, in many earlier accounts, the Kings
were sharply differentiated, with Xerxes in particular marking
a change in direction in the Persian 'policy' of toleration. New
readings of the evidence – in particular of the notorious 'daiva'
inscription in which Xerxes appears to describe his destruction of foreign shrines – have suggested a far greater degree of
continuity.[3] In general, then, far from the picture of some
earlier accounts of a remote, rapacious and violent despotism, the Persian empire is now commonly portrayed as
relatively benign towards its subject peoples, especially by
comparison with its Assyrian and Babylonian predecessors –
though scholars have not lost sight of the underlying reali-
ties of Persian power. In the words of Heleen Sancisi-
Weerdenburg:[4]

> I do not want to argue that the effects of the Persian
> empire on its subject populations were either better or
> worse than those of previous or later Near Eastern em-
> pires ... [But] the term 'Oriental Despotism' carries with
> it value-ridden connotations. It suggests harshness,
> autocracy, and stagnation. It essentially is a verdict, not
> a descriptive model.

This repositioning of the Persian empire – the move, in
particular, beyond clichéd assumptions of Oriental despotism

– is, in broad terms, a thoroughly positive development. There is perhaps a danger, however, reflected in some recent accounts (others, it should be insisted, hold out for the centrality of violent power to Persian imperialism) of our merely shifting from a default assumption of decadence and despotism to an assumption instead of tolerance, openness and the popularity of the empire with its subjects. A positive narrative of Persian imperialism has arguably become so entrenched that contrary currents of evidence are now *understated*.

We begin with the most notorious negative portrayal of Persian imperial power, the representation of Cambyses' occupation of Egypt. Herodotus' account of Cambyses is a catalogue of excess and violence, but one charge perhaps stands out: the accusation that Cambyses murdered the Apis calf, believed to be the incarnation of the god.[5] It is this episode, together with other instances of Cambyses' sacrilege in Egypt – his mocking and burning of cult images, for example – that prompts Herodotus' famous pronouncement that Cambyses must have been mad to mock the customs of others, and his account of Darius' illustration of every culture's attachment to their own customs.[6] Egyptian sources, however, suggest that an Apis calf was buried with full honours in 524 BC, right in the period of the Persian occupation.[7] The terminology of an inscription suggests not only that Cambyses participated in the funeral rites of Apis, but that he did so in the formal capacity of a king of upper and lower Egypt. In the words of Pierre Briant, 'Cambyses was a conqueror seeking to take his place and his rank in the rites and rituals of the Egyptians; he was an Achaemenid king who wished to comply, as pharaoh, with the practices and beliefs that had become inscribed in the Egyptian *longue durée*.'[8] The autobiographical account of one élite Egyptian who came to an accommodation with the Persian occupiers broadens this picture out significantly. Udjahorresnet gives himself credit – immodesty is a function of the genre in which he was writing[9] – for bringing Cambyses round to a recognition of the 'greatness of Sais', and in particular to the temple of Neith, where this account was inscribed on a statue of himself. Again, then, Cambyses appears in a more positive light: adjusting, under local guidance, to the expectations of his Egyptian subjects.

The evidence does not, however, point quite so uniformly in one direction. 'It is important to redress the balance, but not to overreact', in the words of Christopher Tuplin.[10] The records of the burials of Apis calves, as other scholars have pointed out, give legitimate room for (at least some residual) doubt. Particularly difficult to explain is a long gap of a year and a half between the death of one Apis and the birth of a subsequent one, a gap into which another Apis – whose installation provoked Cambyses, as in Herodotus' account – might just be fitted.[11] (Establishing a firm chronology of the period of Cambyses' occupation is notoriously difficult.[12]) The existence of similar stories ascribed to other figures in Egyptian history[13] – together with the general picture of pragmatic accommodation conveyed by the Udjahorresnet inscription – may still suggest that the accusation was one readily thrown at any 'bad ruler'. Cambyses' 'bad press' may plausibly be explained either as a result of a *damnatio memoriae* under his successor Darius or of his curtailing of Egyptian temple income. (A later Egyptian chronicle records him as having stopped gifts of poultry to the temples with the words: 'give them geese no longer; the priests should raise geese themselves ...'[14]) But the case of the Apis calf is not one that can be definitively closed.

Perhaps more significant, however, in terms of exposing the initial difficulties of Cambyses' rule in Egypt, is the Udjahorresnet inscription. Udjahorresnet's role in leading Cambyses to a proper appreciation of the 'greatness of Sais' is all the more significant in his account for following on from a period of crisis. Not only had 'foreigners ... set themselves down in the temple of Neith', but Udjahorresnet talks also of a 'very great disaster':[15]

> I was an orderly man in this city. I saved its people from the very great disaster, which befell in the entire land. There was not its like in this land. I protected the weak from the strong. I saved the fearful on the day of his misfortune. I did for them everything useful, when the time came to do it ... I did for them everything useful as a father does for his son, when the disaster befell in this nome, at the time of the very great disaster which fell out in this entire land.

The text needs to be read in the context of its dedication: it is concerned with Udjahorresnet's individual virtue, and swings from abstraction to apparently concrete biography. Connecting the 'disaster' to the initial aftermath of Cambyses' invasion, rather than to a rebellion early in the reign of Darius, depends on a complex argument over the order in which the different passages of text on the statue should be read.[16] Udjahorresnet, moreover, had an ulterior motive, arguably, in building up the initial disruption of the Persian occupation so as to maximise his own role in mitigating it. On the other hand, it is perhaps perverse to rule out, or too energetically to minimise, a significant degree of initial disruption in the immediate aftermath of the occupation. (Heleen Sancisi-Weerdenburg, for example, described Cambyses' curtailing of temple revenues as 'the only evidence of inconsiderate behaviour'.[17]) There are practical reasons why an occupying army might think to squat within temple precincts.[18] Pierre Briant, by contrast, is noticeably realistic in his response to Udjahorresnet's testimony, citing the destruction of Egyptian temples on the southern frontier at Elephantine, as well as in the Delta, and '[imagining] that many other instances of outrage against both goods and persons were perpetrated by the troops'.[19]

Some inconsiderateness, indeed, can only be expected in the context of an invasion. Xerxes' suppression of revolt in Babylon presents some similar issues. The argument of Amélie Kuhrt and Susan Sherwin-White, that Xerxes' theft of the cult image of Bel-Marduk was based on a misreading of Herodotus' account, is incontrovertible.[20] Whether, however, a Babylonian revolt might have been met with *some* targeted response is a separate question.[21] Evidence for some such response may indeed have been identified: the ziqqurat of Marduk in Babylon shows signs of an attempt fatally to undermine its structure, a deliberate act of sabotage that, it has been argued, can best be dated to the reign of Xerxes.[22] In the light of other such targeted responses (not least, for example, the expedition against Athens and Eretria, culminating in Marathon), this proposition should not perhaps seem surprising.[23] The sudden falling-off in the quantity of Babylonian archival material, at exactly the same time as the revolt from Xerxes' rule, has also plausibly been taken to suggest a causal connection: that the revolt's suppression caused significant disruption to temple archives and to the Babylonian aristocracy.[24]

It is crucial also to consider the spirit in which such violence took place. As Briant again has pointed out in the context of Cambyses' occupation of Egypt, 'it would be an error to see this as the manifestation of an anti-Egyptian policy; it was simply the prerogative of the victors'.[25] (Cyrus too had, in the same vein, sent temple treasures to Persia from Ecbatana and Sardis.) Though some violence may have been indiscriminate, parallels to other Persian campaigns (the attitude to Greek cults of Xerxes, for example[26]) suggests that it might, to a significant degree, have been targeted. There are signs that Egypt's new Persian rulers attempted to stress continuity from Amasis' usurped predecessor Apries, and to bypass and damn Amasis (if so, it is possible that some of the traditions concerning the abuse of Amasis' body have some historical basis).[27] It is very possible also that some of Cambyses' actions were reprisals against those temples which had not acted quickly to legitimise his kingship.[28] In short, the picture was inevitably a mixed one. Both acts of violence and restraint, both the removal and the restoration of temple privileges, are means to the same end: effective domination. And similar pragmatic concerns would have dominated the thoughts of Egyptian survivors like Udjahorresnet.[29] 'The allegiance of Udjahorresnet himself was won conditionally', according to Briant: 'he would not have recognized Cambyses' power unless Cambyses had adopted the rules and precepts of traditional pharaonic royalty'.[30] But how strong a bargaining position was he in? As Michel Austin has asserted in the context of the Seleucid empire, the 'degree of loyalty or resistance to Seleukid rule ... will have depended on circumstances and the balance of pressures at any given time'.[31] More broadly, the attitudes of Egyptians towards foreign conquest are likely to have varied, to have evolved, and to have been complex, even contradictory.[32] To suppose that a foreign king would have seemed unproblematic only so long as the king in question conformed to the outward requirements of the religious role of Pharaoh may be to reduce the Egyptians to a caricature.[33]

More broadly, this pragmatic focus should force us to reconsider the Persians' reputation for (what is usually termed) 'religious tolerance'. Discussion of this aspect of Persian imperialism has often centred around one text, the so-called 'daiva inscription' of Xerxes, in which the King describes his destruction of the shrines of some demons or 'daivas':[34]

And among those countries there were (some) where formerly the daivas had been worshipped. Afterwards by the favour of Ahuramazda I destroyed that place of the daivas, and I gave orders: 'The daivas shall not be worshipped any longer!' Wherever formerly the daivas have been worshipped, there I worshipped Ahuramazda at the proper time and with the proper ceremony.

This declaration was in the past seen by some scholars as marking a departure on Xerxes' part from the policy of toleration of his predecessors, another symptom of the general decline which that King had initiated.[35] Recent work, however, has pointed out the ahistorical nature of the text:[36] that, far from specifying a particular location for the 'daivas', or even referring to any specific occasion, the text is making a more general point, warning against rebellion from royal power. It may not quite be the case to say that the worship of daivas 'describes' rebellion,[37] but it is at least a reasonable deduction from the fact of rebellion. Moreover, though Xerxes worships Ahuramazda on the site of the demons' own worship, he does not, it has been pointed out, require others to do the same:[38] he is not proselytising or imposing Persian gods on their subject peoples.

Without our reverting to old readings of the daiva text, however, which saw it as evidence of a departure in religious policy on Xerxes' part, it may be possible to go too far in reducing its words to *mere* abstraction. Though the inscription may not refer to any actual destruction of temples, no one will seriously doubt that such destruction took place. In Herodotus' account of the climax of the Ionian revolt, for example, the Persians' threats were realised: not only was the male population of Miletus killed, its women and children sold into slavery, but the temple of Apollo at Didyma was plundered and burnt.[39] The main point of discussion, perhaps, should be what *animated* such actions on the part of the Persian Kings. One recent account describes the sacking of the Athenian Acropolis (and the carrying away of statues from the Acropolis and Agora) in swashbuckling terms as the Persians 'finally delivering the punishment for [the Athenians'] disloyalty'.[40] What matters is that such actions constitute a 'measure taken against rebellion, not a punishment of deviating religious behaviour', according to Sancisi-Weerdenburg.[41] '[I]ncidental punitive measures taken against local sanctuaries always were politically, not religiously motivated', in the words of Wouter Henkelman.[42] Leaving aside the likely anachronism of such a hard-and-fast distinction, it is surely a significant fact that any act of rebellion is conceived as a kind of ontological rebellion. (This mildly messianic tone – or, at least, highly commanding religious flavour – to Persian imperial ideology is, in fact, well captured by our Greek sources.[43])

The best reason perhaps why Xerxes should not be seen as departing from a Persian policy of religious tolerance is that such a policy never existed in the first place. Some contemporary scholars refer, for example, to a 'policy of accepting and supporting foreign cults and religions',[44] but the inappropriateness of the term 'tolerance' was clearly recognised nearly thirty years ago by the pioneer of the Achaemenid History Workshops, Heleen Sancisi-Weerdenburg. 'Tolerancy [is] itself an anachronistic concept' she wrote as early as 1982 (in her notice on the first Achaemenid 'colloquium').[45] The reasons why tolerance is an anachronistic term emerge from her summary of the paper at that colloquium of R.J. van der Spek: 'In the polytheistic mind every god, even the god of the most hated enemy, can exist and have power, and it is therefore better to remain on good terms with every god.'[46] When Darius wrote to Gadatas, warning him not to abuse land sacred to Apollo, the 'god who spoke every exactitude to the Persians', the same instinct seems to have been at worked, backed up with some administrative zeal.[47] (Casting doubt on the appropriateness of the term 'tolerance' is not to suggest that there was not a deliberate quality to the Kings' actions in the religious sphere.[48]) Consequently also, to applaud the Persians for not proselytising, for not imposing their own cults more broadly, is to give them credit for something that they could scarcely have thought to do.

The same point applies to the Persians' reputation for tolerance or openness more broadly. Just as they are sometimes defended, in the case of Xerxes' or Cambyses' actions in Babylon or Egypt, from the charge of doing perhaps what any conqueror would do, they are also arguably given credit for *not* doing what they could not have done. The Persians, according to Maria Brosius, 'had no wish to impose their language, culture and religion on their subjects, and instead allowed each ethnic group to retain its cultural identity and heritage'.[49] But, though they might perhaps have chosen to assert a single language for imperial administration, or expected some form of lip service paid to their divinities, the Persian Kings could no more have imposed Old Persian on their subjects than the European Union could impose the continental breakfast. If Persian administration continued to be multilingual, it was primarily on pragmatic grounds. Likewise, as Brosius acknowledges, to the extent that the Persian Kings 'allowed' the peoples of the empire to maintain their identity (or refrained from making vain attempts at suppressing it) they did so as a matter of 'political expediency', to '[limit] regional opposition and rebellion'.[50] As Margaret Cool Root has written, 'we perhaps frequently err in a tacit assumption that the Achaemenids would have liked to assert a policy of pan-Persianism'.[51]

Can the Persian empire, or Persian imperial ideology, meaningfully be described as inclusive then? To term it inclusive should surely imply more than simply the 'allowing' of a diversity of cultures, 'something like a doctrine of minimal interference and "live and let live"'.[52] For example, it might be merited on the basis of their positive investment in the distinct cultures of their subject peoples, or their inviting those peoples to share in the benefits of empire. There is little clear evidence of either. The lists of the King's subject peoples included in royal inscriptions, like the iconographic details of the delegates at the Apadana, undoubtedly take relish in the token characteristics of each people in turn (the pointed-cap Scythians, and so on). But the prime reason for these lists is not, surely, to celebrate the multicultural diversity of the Persian empire, but as a demonstration of the King's power. In the words of Amélie Kuhrt:[53]

> When the kings emphasize the diversity of the groups which make up their empire, the effect is to enhance the supreme and absolute power of the Persian monarch, who has such vast, variegated resources at his command and is able to unite them in his service.

The Persian empire, undoubtedly, drew upon the skills of its subject peoples, it engaged with their local traditions, it sought to speak to them in terms that they could readily accommodate. At the same time, however, it was a pronouncedly Persocentric world: in which a Persian elite dominated (both the court and the satrapies)[54] and the 'Persian man' was elevated for his ideal qualities. And the empire, like any other, existed also for the exploitation of its subjects. 'Imperial administration concerns above all two things', as Christopher

Tuplin puts it soberly: 'the extraction of profit for the ruling power and the maintenance of control (and hence of the possibility of exploitation)'.[55]

Against this background, any attempt to find the subject peoples of the empire *identifying* with an imperial ideology or mission appears like hopeless wishful thinking. It has been suggested, for example, that the idealised list of the skills of different peoples in the Susa Foundation Charter may have been designed also 'to ignite the pride of different ethnic groups in their participation', but this is a reaction on the part of the peoples in question that is predicated on a clear prior identification with Persian rule – itself unproven and perhaps inherently unlikely.[56] Carl Nylander has described the imperial art of Persepolis as creating a a 'kind of "palais des nations", a building to which every visitor can somehow relate and in which he can feel a bit at home, by means of significant, well known architectural and decorative forms transferred from his own environment'.[57] 'We seem to see empire also from the peoples' point of view and we sense a notion almost of a commonwealth.'[58] Another scholar has gone further in developing the thesis of the economic benefits derived from a shared imperial ideology.[59] And yet, just as recent Achaemenid historians have emphasised that Greek sources on Persia are often in fact writing (through Persian fantasies) about their own worlds,[60] there is a clear danger that we end up seduced by the perspective of Persian imperial ideology. (If we sought to glean the view of British imperial subjects solely from the imperial art of London, we would find evidence, similarly, of an 'ideology of commonwealth' – but we would scarcely credit it as representative.) The manner in which, in Persian iconography, the peoples of the empire hold up the throne of the King with their finger tips, as if their burden were a happy one, has been seen as an expression of their joyous assent to royal power: an ideological statement certainly, but a statement of the subjects' support of, their investment in, royal power (see Figs 8-9).[61] And yet, in one instance in which this image of the enthroned king on a platform, supported by his imperial subjects, is accompanied by a text – on the tomb of Darius – the accompanying text puts the accent very firmly on the brazen statement of royal power:[62]

> By the favour of Ahuramazda these are the countries which I seized outside of Persia; I ruled over them; they bore tribute to me; what was said to them by me, that they did; my law – that held them firm ... If now you shall think that 'How many are the countries which King Darius held?' look at the sculptures (of those) who bear the throne, then shall you know, then shall it become known to you: the spear of a Persian man has gone forth far; then shall it become known to you: a Persian man has delivered battle far indeed from Persia.

Even so, it has been maintained, Persian royal iconography is markedly free of scenes of violence: the King on his throne, or with a parasol held up above him (see Fig. 3), is a long way from the images of hunting or conquest of their Near Eastern predecessors.[63] 'The only violent depiction seen in Persepolis', it has been written, 'is that of the royal hero in combat with a wild beast, but the royal hero is already victorious, because the beast has been mortally wounded by his dagger.'[64] The impli-

4. *Live and Let Live*

Fig. 8. The tomb of Darius at Naqsh-i-Rustam: detail, with the King held aloft by the peoples of the empire, and with tomb inscription.

Fig. 9. Naqsh-i-Rustam: the royal tombs of the Achaemenids (and of later Sasanian kings).

cation might be taken away that this is fundamentally a peaceful world, built on imagined consent more than violence. And yet violence lurks only slightly beneath the polished surface.[65] In the ahistorical world of Persian iconography, a *narrative* account in sculptural form of the conquest of x or y people would have been impossible:[66] the repeated images of the royal hero triumphant, on the verge of plunging a dagger into a monstrous opponent, do not gloss over violence but on the contrary show the inevitability of the King's victory – a 'message of power and assertive protection', in Root's fine phrase[67] – just as the processing subjects of the Apadana reliefs illustrate the naturalness of submission to his power. In Root's words again, 'A teasing relationship between space and time is created here by depicting delegates who are *about to be* led forward to offer their gifts'; the violence likewise is *imminent* (see Figs 1 and 4).[68]

This pattern of scholars *wishing* Persia's imperial subjects to have a positive attitude towards Persian rule is evident not only in the interpretation of imperial art and inscriptions but also (in ample examples) in the context of historical narrative. Herodotus' story, for example, of the death of the satrap Oroites – that he was killed by his guards, out of automatic obedience to the written command of the King, Darius – has been interpreted by Briant (despite its 'fictionalized and bombastic tone') as apparently 'revealing' of the real relations between King and subjects.[69]

Reading Herodotus' account does not leave us with the impression that Oroetes would have found many Persians at Sardis ready to follow him in his rebellion. For them, loyalty to the monarchy consisted of the desire to preserve all of the privileges that accrued to them from imperial dominion.

The underlying historical hypothesis here, of a strong inter-dependence of monarchy and elite, may well be a valid one. What needs to be underlined, however, is that Herodotus' tale is an expression of an *ideology* of loyalty to the King; it is not evidence of actual loyalty.

Likewise, Briant and others have shown, arguably, an incli-nation to *minimise* the extent of anti-Persian feeling beneath the Ionian revolt,[70] say, or in response to the Persian expedi-tions to Greece. From their initial campaign in the islands of the Aegean before Marathon, the Persians found confirmation that 'in fact, in the face of Persian aggression, the Greeks did not have a unified patriotic hatred of "barbarians"'.[71] But this is, in essence, to demolish a straw man.[72] The fact, conversely, that two rich Eretrians betrayed their city to the Persians (to use emotive terms) in no way disproves a *widespread* hostility to 'barbarians': it may, especially as the barbarians were at the gates in armed force, have been an expression of opportunism, or of a *mixed* response.[73] A complex response to imperial power, indeed – subtle forms of cultural resistance operating alongside political submission – is of course amply evidenced in other contexts. Erich Gruen has identified similar patterns of resistance even in the ostensibly positive accounts of Persian rule in biblical sources. Jewish sources on Persia, he has found, 'resonate with disparagement rather than deference':[74]

They [the Jews] claimed Cyrus' victories as exhibiting the

power of Yahweh, they tied Persian policy to the laws of Moses, they represented royal actions as reliant upon Jewish initiative, and they held kings up to mockery. The Achaemenids might rule an empire, but they borrowed their moral and intellectual authority from the Jews.

We should not be surprised to find, indeed we should *expect* to find, similar attitudes – between disparagement and deference, between identification and distancing, or indeed holding these contrary positions *simultaneously* – in other contexts.

Persian royal ideology, likewise, contains a complex mix of attitudes: the hope of peaceful, graceful convergence, of joyous assent to royal power, the expectation of submission, the threat and advertisement of force. The Kings' bold assertion of their own power over their subject peoples perhaps receives less attention than it might, by comparison with the more positive currents of royal ideology. The words of Darius' tomb inscription (quoted above) or of the inscription of Darius at Suez – with its 'tone of national pride and imperial arrogance', in the words of Alan Lloyd[75] – should perhaps provide a corrective to any too rose-tinted view of Persian imperialism. In the words of the latter:[76]

> Saith Darius the king: I am a Persian; from Persia I seized Egypt; I gave order to dig this canal from a river by name Nile which flows in Egypt, to the sea which goes from Persia. Afterwards this canal was dug thus as I had ordered, and ships went from Egypt through the canal to Persia, thus as was my desire.

5

Terra Incognita

What I want to say is simply that, taken in its entirety and
not reduced to the study of a few major sites ..., and
despite the attempt at synthesis by Olmstead in 1948 that
continues to deserve our respect, the history of the
Achaemenid empire remained largely *terra incognita*.

Pierre Briant (2002: 4)

We turn now to another issue, the intellectual genealogy of the
modern study of Achaemenid Persia, and whether – to put it
at its most blunt – previous scholarship is as bad, or as
Hellenocentric, as it is often presented as being. No one, of
course, would seriously suggest that the modern historiography of Persia began from a clean slate in 1980 (and the
initiation of the Achaemenid History Workshops). The renaissance in Achaemenid history that was consolidated and gath-
ered pace in the 1980s in fact began at least a decade earlier,
as Briant himself acknowledged at the time.[1] (It is probably
impossible to pin down the causes of this renewed interest:
Hallock's landmark publication of the fortification tablets,[2] or
even the Shah's celebration of the 2500th anniversary of the
empire[3] may both have lit fuses.) However, it is easy to
imagine, from the tone of much that has been published since,

that the beginning of the workshops marked a more profound caesura, or to suppose that the Hellenocentric version of our Greek sources was swallowed whole by previous historians.[4] Early travellers and historians tend, at best, to be given credit for adding to the sum of our knowledge, especially of monuments, not for their interpretative framework.[5] The model of Persian decadence remained frozen, according to Amélie Kuhrt and Heleen Sancisi-Weerdenburg,[6] unmoved by the nineteenth-century decipherment of cuneiform or by new excavations: 'The Greeks could not have been too far wrong', they comment (sarcastically): 'they were first of all Greeks, and therefore almost infallible, and secondly, they had been contemporaries and thus had first-hand knowledge.'

The quantity of previous writing on Persia, and especially on its monuments, is vast. As George Curzon, later viceroy of India, commented in 1892 in the context of an exhaustive review of previous writers (not exclusively on *ancient* Persia):[7]

Few countries so sparsely visited have been responsible for so ample a bibliography. The reason is obvious. To each newcomer the comparative rarity of his experience has been conceded as the excuse for a volume. In the category of these productions are to be found works as painstaking and meritorious as ever passed through the Press. Nor is their value in any degree diminished, it is, on the contrary, enhanced by the fact that the list of which I speak includes some of the most worthless rubbish that has ever blundered into print.

This chapter examines only a relatively small slice of previous historiography: mainly British (and American) writers, pre-dominantly from the late nineteenth and earlier twentieth centuries, and by no means all painstaking or meritorious. What this slice of history- and travel-writing reveals (like the survey of eighteenth-century Greek histories of Maria Brosius[8]) is a very much more complex and, in many instances, a more positive approach to the Achaemenid past than is commonly presented. Whether in detailed research (in the case, say, of Curzon[9]) or in passing impressions (in the case of less academic travellers, most commonly missionaries or soldiers for whom 'antiquarian pursuits were a minority hobby in an overwhelming environment of heat, disease, boredom and excessive drinking'[10]), these writers also in many ways pre-empt the conclusions of more recent scholarship.[11]

It should be stated at the outset: if you look in these earlier writings for signs of the model of decadence and decline identified by the new Achaemenid historians – for stories of harem intrigues or the moral weaknesses of the Persian Kings – you will not be disappointed. George Rawlinson's narrative (in his *Fifth Monarchy*) digests all the unsavoury details of Ctesias and other fragmentary authors of the fourth century, dwelling for example on the moral weakness of Xerxes (with 'scarcely a trait whereon the mind can dwell with any satisfaction'[12]). Similarly, A.T. Olmstead follows Herodotus in lingering on the domestic consequences for Persia of her defeat in the Persian wars, constructing the harem intrigue at the close of Herodotus' account as a turning point in Persian fortunes: 'failure of the European adventure opened the way to harem intrigues, with all their deadly consequences'.[13]

Indeed 'harem intrigues' are sufficiently common in Olmstead's text as to warrant an index entry.

The detailed histories of Olmstead and Rawlinson are rare instances, however, of such a clear formulation of the 'thesis' of Persian decline. (It is perhaps not coincidental indeed that they have so frequently been latched onto by recent scholars: together with J.M. Cook, whose history of the Persian empire had the misfortune of being published just as the tide of new Achaemenid history was rising,[14] these two writers have become emblematic of a pejorative, Hellenocentric view of ancient Persia.[15]) For the most part, decadence and decline, though they appear as leitmotifs in many narratives, emerge as impersonal processes without significant landmarks or elaboration: the thesis of Persian decline from 479 can, after all, only really be sustained by a giant act of elision. A number of authors make the point that no one could have foretold Persian decline, that the Persian wars could only be recognised as a turning point with hindsight. 'The mischief was internal', according to G.B. Grundy: 'it was situate far away in the depths of Asia, beyond the ken of the Greek of the fifth century, and it is not strange that he never appreciated the full extent of the malady'[16] – and therefore it is somehow beyond our ken too, beyond explanation or clear identification. Signs of weakness are sometimes mentioned without being clearly identified.[17] Alternatively a narrative of progressive decadence is *presumed*. So, for example, when the American traveller-historian A.V. Williams Jackson is offered water from a goat-skin tankard, this leads him – meanderingly – to an observation on the Achaemenids:[18]

These rude vessels were made from the undressed hide of a goat, with the animal's hair left on the outside and the skin drawn tightly around a wooden rim and a circular board bottom so as to form a bucket, while three sticks were used as fastenings to give firmness to the whole and as props for the uncouth vessel to stand upon. I presume it was from tankards such as these that the hardy soldiers of Cyrus used to drink, before luxury taught them the use of silver beakers and the accompanying vices which sapped away the vigor that had conquered kingdoms.

At the same time, other writers in fact prefigure recent views. The soldier-historian Percy Sykes, for example, insists that Persia 'played the leading part in the history of the known world' for the 150 years after Salamis (decadence does, like a 'dry rot', creep in, in the figures of women and eunuchs, but only late on – in the court of Darius III[19]). Sykes also makes the argument, again familiar from recent histories, that to assume the Persian empire decadent robs Alexander of credit for his military achievement.[20] (This is a long way, then, from the image of Persia as frozen in decadence from the time of the Persian wars or from the death of Xerxes, or of Alexander's campaigns as a mercy killing.[21])

There is a similar spread of responses to imperial Persian art and architecture. Again, of course, there are negative judgements. John Macdonald Kinneir or George Rawlinson are distinctly churlish: Kinneir damning Persian sculpture (though finding Persepolis 'one of … the most magnificent structures, that art has ever raised to the glory and admiration of mankind'),[22] Rawlinson finding nothing in either sculpture or architecture 'indicative of any remarkable artistic genius'.[23] Such negative views, however, are in general exceptions to a rule of ecstasy: as one disappointed British traveller admits, the reason for his disappointment at Persepolis was probably 'the fact that it has been crammed down my throat, upon every available occasion, ever since I landed in Persia'.[24] 'Standing in the gathering twilight in front of the vast platform', the colonial official Bradley-Birt wrote (to give just one example), 'the modern Western mind half fails to grasp the thought of so much splendour and antiquity.'[25]

Again, moreover, a number of writers foreshadow trends in more recent scholarship. Far, for example, from sharing the damning judgement of Bernard Berenson on Achaemenid art (that it displayed the 'originality of incompetence'[26]) a number of writers foreshadow the work of Carl Nylander or of Margaret Cool Root in emphasising the extent to which Achaemenid art combined and added a twist to its various models, Greek, Babylonian or Egyptian.[27] This number in-cludes both fairly serious figures and more passing, less academic travellers. For Curzon, for example, the relationship of Persian and other art is a major issue to which he devotes a lengthy and learned discussion: 'while [Persia] borrowed much' he concludes, 'she also added something of her own, enough, beyond all question, to lift her art from the rank of a purely imitative or servile school'.[28] The American financial administrator A.C. Millspaugh, on the other hand, with only a little self-interest, found that the Persians have always 'had a rare capacity for drawing on the special gifts of other peoples without losing their own characteristics and integrity'.[29] The doctor Rosalie Morton took a sentimental view of the work being done by artists brought back from foreign conquests: their 'captivity was lightened by congenial work and by comradeship, for here the genius of the then known world was brought together and flowered'.[30]

Other aspects of modern interpretations of Persepolis are also foreshadowed. Writers as diverse as Percy Sykes or the English doctor Treacher Collins (a consultant to a Qajar prince, who sees himself as a modern Democedes of Croton) both understand that the apparent sameness of Persepolitan sculpture is intentional, that it reflects in Treacher Collins' words 'a oneness in composition which is exceedingly remarkable'.[31] Curzon draws a parallel between the processions of the Apadana and the Panathenaia.[32] And some writers develop the broader thesis of Persian influence on Greek art and culture. 'All that is Ionic in the arts of Greece is derived from the valleys of the Tigris and the Euphrates.'[33] The American diplomat S.G.W. Benjamin sees the origins of Greek music in Persia.[34] Even George Rawlinson contemplates the possibility of Persian influence on Greek art.[35] In short, the body of work that Nylander and Margaret Root were reacting against may not have been an aberration, but nonetheless represented only one strand in the history of previous writing on Persian art.[36] Indeed, when Gisela Richter expressed her thesis of the Greek character of Persian art (citing the Susa Foundation Charter as final proof), it seems clear that she was aware of the relative novelty of her position. Only years before, a monumental survey of Persian art under the direction of the influential Arthur Upham Pope enshrined a very different set of views. 'It is above all the quality and spirit of Achaemenid art', according to Pope, 'that set at naught this theory of imitation or mere eclecticism. Wholly new values are in control.'[37] Other contributors reformulate the same position,[38] emphasise the close control of foreign artists or that the Ionians of the Foundation Charter are 'workmen and technicians',[39] or – most strikingly in terms of recent concerns – cast doubt on the term 'Graeco-Persian': 'the coinage of the term … is unfortunate, since it either begs the question at issue or conveys nothing', according to Casson;[40] 'one still occasionally finds Achaemenid seals called "Graeco-Persian"', R.S. Cooke observes regretfully.[41]

Many writers of these earlier periods indeed go further than modern scholars in a powerful, if sometimes politically freighted, *identification* with ancient Persia. In many regards, Persia and the Persians are often assumed to be frozen in an undeveloped state. As Sir John Malcolm, three times an ambassador to the Persian court at the turn of the nineteenth century, remarks rather paradoxically in conclusion to his 1815 *History of Persia*: 'Though no country has undergone, during the last twenty centuries, more revolutions than the kingdom of Persia, there is, perhaps, none that is less altered in its condition.'[42] This assumption of continuity allows for the construction of an extraordinarily consistent set of ethnographic commonplaces:[43] on the one hand, humorous and quick[44] and of 'agreeable and prepossessing manners',[45] the Persians (or more broadly 'Orientals') are also deceitful,[46] vain, envious, greedy,[47] uncontrolled in the expression of their emotions[48] – and, 'compelled, by the nature of their government, … alternately submissive and tyrannical'.[49] (Many of these stereotypes, interestingly, live on.[50])

In certain areas, however, this assumption of continuity

breaks down, and allows for an engagement with the ancient Persians which is unmediated (at least superficially) by contemporary experience, by which the British reach over the heads, as it were, of the modern Iranians, 'redirect[ing] their attentions away from the living Orient, reinvesting them in the ancient one'.[51] One such area is (ancient) Zoroastrian religion:[52] 'of a more elevated character than is usual with races not enlightened by special revelation ...', according to the Anglican canon George Rawlinson, a 'pure spiritual monotheism'.[53] (Counter-evidence to the thesis of Persian monotheism is put down to a decline from pure beginnings, rather than leading to the questioning of their Zoroastrianism, as in more recent accounts.[54]) This admiration for Persian monotheism is clearly in part the result of Cyrus' biblical image: 'a religious sympathy seems to have drawn together the two nations of the Persians and the Jews', according to Rawlinson again.[55] Zoroastrianism is not, however, only a symptom of moral discrimination – the reflection of an 'attempt to account for the coexistence of good and evil', in the words of Ross[56] – but interestingly also seen as a *cause* of empire. '[When] their religion with its lofty and sane ideals is taken into consideration', according to Sykes, 'it is little wonder that these enlightened Aryans founded an empire and held in subjection the lower Semitic and Turanian races whose civilization they had absorbed.'[57] '[The Medes and Persians] had qualities which raised them above their fellows', George Rawlinson grudgingly admits, 'and a civilization, which was not, perhaps, very advanced, but was still not wholly contemptible.'[58]

It is, however, more than any other area, in the history of the built remains of the Achaemenid past that continuity between ancient and modern Persia is seen to have collapsed. All visitors to Persepolis and other Persian sites share an overwhelming sense of pathos. 'How do the old cities sink into the earth and disappear?', lamented E.R. Durand, wife of the British Minister Sir Mortimer Durand.[59] Persepolis, according to Bradley-Birt, 'is a scene of utter desolation, pillars broken and cast down, columns shorn of their summits, pedestals bereft of their columns, mournful, neglected, and pathetic, yet magnificent and proud, with all the pride of a greatness that has passed away'.[60] Later he speaks of their 'majesty in decay, their mute triumphant protest against the warring hand of time and man'.[61] Williams Jackson, conversely, finds at Ecbatana no 'trace of that solemn grandeur which is noble in its decay at Persepolis or Pasargadae'.[62]

Such phrases are reminiscent of the climax of Margaret Cool Root's monograph, where the image of the four quarters singing harmonious praise to the King at Persepolis is described as 'a haunting finale to the pre-Hellenic east'.[63] Where they differ, however, is in their biting criticism of the modern-day Persians for failing to appreciate their heritage. 'The love of travel, visiting the remains of former grandeur, and of tracing the history of ancient nations, which is so common in Europe, causes wonder in the Asiatics, amongst whom there is little or no spirit of curiosity or speculation', according to Sir John Malcolm.[64] 'These people seem to take no pride and interest in their antiquities', according to Valentine Baker.[65] 'The modern Persian, unmindful of its wonder and its beauty, still carelessly calls Persepolis by the name of the Takht-i-Jamshid, the Throne of Jamshid, ascribing to the popular hero anything the origin of which is obscure or too much trouble to discover' – according to Bradley-Birt.[66] The tone of condescension becomes sharper still in the context of the tomb of Cyrus (see Fig. 6). 'There is a mockery in the fact that it is now known as the Tomb of the Mother of Solomon, and is surrounded by the graves of Muslims', according to the American Benjamin Burges Moore.[67] 'Such is the sepulchre of the King of Kings to-day. But let it not be imagined that its story is known to the inhabitants of the country … Always he appears to prefer legend to history and superstition to both.'[68] (Edward Granville Browne is rare in citing Persian observations on the pathos of Persepolis.[69])

The identity of the rightful inheritors of Cyrus and Darius – those who appreciate their works – scarcely needs spelling out. But this is not only a matter of artistic appreciation. The 'desolation' of Persepolis is only representative of Persia's more general decline from her ancient greatness.[70] 'How they have fallen from their first estate, my reminiscences wofully show', according to George Fowler (an English traveller in 1841).[71] 'The Persia of Herodotus and Xenophon was immeasurably superior to Mediaeval Persia in its attributes and is even now more respectable in its ruins', according to George Curzon.[72] Persia, according to Valentine Baker, had 'fallen through misgovernment and corruption to almost the lowest point which a once great nation can reach without dissolution'.[73] Bradley-Birt takes his readers on a procession through all the great periods of Persian history before one descends with a crashing thud into the modern era:[74]

No country in the world can boast a prouder or more ancient history than this land of the King of Kings …

Cyrus the Achaemenian, and Darius the son of Hystaspes, Shapur the Sassanian, proud conqueror of the
Roman emperor Valerian, Jenghiz Khan, Tamerlane and
Nadir Shah, empire builders all, Shah Abbas the Sefavi,
and Fath Ali Shah, the Kajar monarch, all pass in the
prime of life and splendour in one long pageant across
the page of Persian history; and at the end of all the
brilliant line there stands the feeble figure of the present
Shah-in-Shah, the unhappy successor of the King of
Kings.

It is a terrible descent from the past to the present.
Dishonesty and corruption have bitten deep into official
life and sapped its strength ... Nothing could well be
more in the style of comic opera than suddenly to spring
a constitution and a representative assembly on a people
who for endless centuries have done nothing but obey ...
A paternal despotism is undoubtedly all that Persia is fit
for to-day.

It was, of course, paternal despotism that had been the secret
of the Persians' earlier success, as a number of authors make
clear. 'With Orientals everything depends upon their leaders',
according to the first American Minister in Persia, S.G.W.
Benjamin.[75] 'An ordinary Oriental', comments Rawlinson in
similar vein, 'would have been content with such a result
[merely becoming king], and have declined to tempt fortune
any more. But Cyrus was no ordinary Oriental.'[76] More often
than not, however, it is the 'uniform civil administration'[77] of
Darius that excites admiration – and identification. 'Bent on
settling and consolidating his Empire', according to Rawlin-

son, 'he set up everywhere the satrapial form of government, organized and established his posts, issued his coinage, watched over the administration, and in various ways, exhibited a love of order and method, and a genius for systematic arrangement.'[78] The identification is even stronger, perhaps unsurprisingly, in the case of the flawed imperial hero Percy Sykes (whose history is dedicated 'to British administrators in India and at Whitehall'), in particular in the kind of things he praises in the Achaemenids (many of which map neatly onto modern travellers' preoccupations[79]): the Kings' construction of a network of roads, the building up of trade links, and above all the empire's vast extent.[80]

No matter the extent of identification, however, between these writers and the imperial Persian past, perhaps the acid test is to ask how Achaemenid Persia measures up against the classical Greco-Roman world – with which they were in most cases thoroughly imbued.

In many cases, predictably, the choice between classical Greece and Persia is a fairly easy one. (Of course, it need not be a choice.) The author of *The Adventures of Hajji Baba*, J.J. Morier, though his reaction to Persepolis was to yield 'at once to emotions the most lively and the most enraptured', nevertheless finds 'nothing, either in the architecture of the buildings, or in the sculptures and reliefs on the rocks, which could bear a critical comparison with the delicate proportions and perfect statuary of the Greeks' – though he adds then that this is perhaps to '[try] Persepolis by a standard to which it never was amenable'.[81] Curzon mocks such comparisons – in particular, those of Persepolis with Milan Cathedral and Windsor Castle – but he too thinks the Apadana staircase not

as fine as the Propylaea of the Acropolis.[82] For George Rawlinson, as his famous verdict on Persian science makes brutally
clear, the Persians offer little competition: 'Too light and
frivolous, too vivacious, too sensuous for such pursuits, they
left them to the patient Babylonians, and the thoughtful,
many-sided Greeks.'[83]

A second group seems torn between two rival identifica-
tions. Williams Jackson, for example, becomes distracted en
route from Russia to Iran by being taken to the site of the
Prometheus Vinctus: 'For a moment, Greek mythology, classic
reminiscences, and thoughts of college days made me forget
that the land of my quest was Iran, not Hellas.'[84] Most
fascinating, perhaps, in his confusion is Percy Sykes. The
purpose of his writing, he remarks in the preface to his history
of Persia, is not only to be useful to his government, 'by
sketching the national character of a subject people', but also
to represent the 'Persian point of view', both to students of
Greek history and to Persians themselves, to help them to
'realize more fully the splendour of their own history'.[85] He
justifies his writing also in terms of the influence of Persia on
later civilization, but it is an influence that is channelled
through the classical Greco-Roman world.[86] He reverts then
also to a more conventional focus on the freedom-loving
Greeks: 'Nevertheless, in Hellas, were to be found a few
thousand warriors who, preposterous as it might appear, were
destined to repel the collective might of this vast empire ....'[87]
The Persians fought bravely in his account; he even goes so far
as to say that in military terms the importance of the Persian
wars had been exaggerated (the point made by Robert Graves
in his poem 'The Persian version' or by Olmstead in shrinking

the Persian wars into a chapter entitled 'Problems of the Greek frontier',[88] but also much earlier[89]), but for Sykes, that is to forget another dimension: 'the wider aspect of the case, the world aspect ... from this point of view, Marathon, Salamis, and Plataea were victories not only for Greece but for mankind ...'.

It would be wrong, however, to conclude that histories of Persia are univocal in their ultimate adherence to the classical world. There are, thirdly, at least as many anti-classical (or *un*-classical) voices. Henry Rawlinson, the decipherer of cuneiform (and the elder brother of George), though he may have yielded to some extent to the Greek sources in presenting Xerxes in a less flattering light than his father Darius,[90] was fully appreciative of the shortcomings of the Greek sources, praising Herodotus faintly as an 'honest, but not very critical, historian' (whose evidence 'must be received with considerable caution'), or observing how 'with the pardonable predilections of a Greek, he neglected ..., or undervalued, the detail of local wars, and confined his notices accordingly, almost exclusively, to those passages of the Persian arms which referred to Europe or to Asia Minor'.[91] The diplomat Edward Eastwick (writing in 1864) actually ridicules Greek accounts of the Persian wars ('Greece put on her poetical spectacles') and his contemporaries' belief in them: 'how can men in their senses affect to believe all that stuff about the invasion of Xerxes?'[92] The Cambridge Orientalist Edward Granville Browne begins his account of his year of adventure in Persia (the only year of adventure in his life, according to his memoirist[93]) with a rant at the failings of a classical education, its 'general failure to invest the books read with any human, historical or literary interest, or to treat them as expressions of the thoughts, feelings, and aspirations of our fellow-creatures instead of as grammatical treadmills'.[94] By contrast, by working on the Near East he was doing the real thing.

Perhaps the best example of this independence from classical education, however, comes from the age before the decipherment of cuneiform: the author of the first full-length history of Persia in English, Sir John Malcolm (responsible for firing the 17-year-old Henry Rawlinson's interest in Persia when they travelled on the same steamer to India[95]). Greek perspectives on Persia are almost entirely excluded from Malcolm's work. As he wrote to his father from Shiraz in 1800, with the exception of Alexander's conquests, there was 'no fact recorded by the Greeks of which Persian historians make the least mention';[96] he was employing every leisure hour in researches into the history of 'this extraordinary country, with which we are but little acquainted'. As a result of his reliance on 'eastern authors' (in which he was far from exceptional among his contemporaries),[97] for Malcolm, for example, the tradition that Persepolis was indeed the throne of the hero Jamshid finds no contradiction.[98] Whereas George Rawlinson, perhaps unsurprisingly, interpreted the newly discovered cuneiform inscriptions in the light of Greek authors,[99] in Malcolm's work, on the rare occasions that Greek sources do make an appearance (in footnotes), they are invariably seen as secondary.[100] Far from his being a maverick, moreover, Malcolm's history was enormously popular, being greeted by Sir Walter Scott, for example, as 'form[ing] the connecting link between that [the history] of Greece and that of Asia'.[101]

If it is right, finally, that these early writers have in many respects been underestimated, are there not good reasons for this? First, of course, it could not reasonably be claimed that a popular historian like Percy Sykes, let alone some of the travellers mentioned here in passing, deserve serious attention today as historians of Persia – though, of course, they may be interesting in their own right, especially when their views so often coincide with those of more serious scholars. Secondly, and more significantly, it may be that the work even of figures such as George Rawlinson or George Curzon might be considered tainted as a result of the imperial context in which they wrote. The intense identification with Persia revealed by many writers, the claim to be delivering the 'Persian point of view' (a claim arguably that goes back to Ctesias, or indeed to Herodotus),[102] might reasonably be connected with the common British claim to be able to get under the skin, even to impersonate, foreigners.[103] Identification, indeed, tips over into a form of appropriation. Curzon's magnificent *Persia and the Persian Question*, with its geographical surveys intended to be of practical use, constituted – with two other books on India's northern and eastern flanks – a long drawn-out application for the post of viceroy of India. He is graphically open about this imperial context in his introduction:[104]

Turkestan, Afghanistan, Transcaspia, Persia – to many these names breathe only a sense of utter remoteness or a memory of strange vicissitudes and of moribund romance. To me, I confess, they are the pieces on a chessboard upon which is being played out a game for the dominion of the world.

This context frequently casts into a foreign light conclusions which may at first appear similar to those of current scholarship. For George Rawlinson, as for recent Achaemenid historians, Cambyses' actions in Egypt are entirely sane. For Rawlinson, however, they also provide the occasion for a timeless moral: 'The Oriental will generally kiss the hand that smites him, if it only smite him hard enough.'[105] When British scholars understood the fashion in which Persian imperial ideology drew on a variety of models, or when they characterised the Persian empire in terms of the difficulty of bonding so many peoples, languages and religions,[106] it is hard to resist the conclusion that they were helped to these views by unconscious analogy from their own experience. Though they were shaped by this imperial context, however, they cannot be reduced to it.[107] It was not just complacent Eurocentrism that drove Henry Rawlinson, through physical as well as intellectual hardships, to the decipherment of cuneiform; while some scholars may have clung on, regardless, to the classical sources with which they were familiar, others struggled to incorporate new Near Eastern material into their intellectual visions.[108] No scholarship, moreover, is clear of some such political shadows. As Amélie Kuhrt asked in 1991, 'to what extent have we, as European scholars, claimed (and continue to claim) the Achaemenid empire for ourselves, making it a part of our own internal historical debates?'[109] Despite all their failings, and despite the context in which they wrote, in Malcolm, Curzon and even Sykes we have the ancestors of the new Achaemenid historiography. We explore the variety of modern agendas further in the concluding chapter.

6

Concluding Hostilities

The Persian wars are not over yet, and one might be tempted to see in the repeatedly uttered accusations of 'hellenocentrism' and 'iranocentrism' in scholarly literature a sign of continued warfare.

Amélie Kuhrt & Heleen Sancisi-Weerdenburg (1987: ix)

The 2005 British Museum exhibition, *Forgotten Empire*, enshrined – in its emphasis on the empire's resilience, its impact and its tolerance, for example – many of the central tenets of recent scholarship. It also artfully exploited the fragile diplomatic context (so fragile indeed that the loan of artefacts from Tehran was very nearly scuppered at the eleventh hour). 'At this difficult time', as the British Museum director Neil McGregor declared at the time, 'when East-West relations and understanding are at a low ebb, it is instructive to see what a remarkable contribution the ancient Near East has made to the cultural heritage of the world.'[1] In another context, alluding to the ongoing hostilities in Iraq, he talked of the Athenians' need to maintain the negative image of the Persian empire to keep together their 'coalition of the willing'.[2] Many journalists and critics faithfully adapted these modern analogies, and the positive image of the Achaemenids underlying them, into their

109

copy, stressing the tolerance of the Persian empire (noting that the Cyrus Cylinder has been called a declaration of human rights even if not approving that view), the empire's cosmopolitanism or 'multiculturalism', and the role of Greek propaganda or 'spin' in perpetuating Persia's negative image.[3] The Persians may have used violence, one journalist found, but unlike the Assyrians, it was violence as a means to an end.[4]

At the same time, however, the exhibition also elicited a significant backlash against this more positive view of the Persian empire: the Persian empire 'turns out to be as grandiose, luxurious and remotely despotic as Herodotus says it was',[5] according to one critic, while another response found that the exhibition had gone 'too far in emphasising the softer sides of Achaemenid achievements'.[6] More specifically, earlier negative views of Achaemenid art were reprised: the lack of 'humanity' or movement in Achaemenid sculpture,[7] or, according to one blogger, its lack of 'visual pizazz', the fact that 'the stuff in the exhibition was all relentlessly about power and wealth'.[8] In the lack of any Persian development of the ideas of citizenship or of the freedom of the individual, Greek prejudice was found (by Peter Jones) to be justified.[9] For some indeed, the positive portrayal of the Achaemenids, and the emphasis on their negative portrayal, itself appeared to be spin.

In some respects, the exhibition's reception reflected some immediate contemporary concerns: in the analogies drawn with the Iraq war, or in the jarring use of the term multiculturalism. In other regards, however, the range of responses follows a pattern that has proved fairly consistent for over a century. Of course, it would be wrong, as with the uninformed responses of some nineteenth-century travellers, to suggest that all the issues raised in this context merit serious discussion, that historical judgement can reasonably be made on the basis of a kind of *vox pop*. At the same time, the exhibition undeniably provided an interesting moment. The experience of thousands of museum visitors processing past, and being variously impressed by, the wares of an ancient culture placed on display, brings into unusually sharp perspective questions that otherwise might go unexamined: the extent of the Persians' 'contribution', or the status of their empire vis-à-vis others. The popular response, moreover, may not be authoritative, but provides an interesting litmus test of what – in any historical consensus – can and cannot be proven, fixed, beyond doubt; it may also reveal fissures and unchallenged assumptions beneath the surface of our academic narratives.

The scholars of the Achaemenid History Workshops began with the determination to question the overarching narrative of Hellenocentrism which, they claimed, had so dominated the understanding of the Persian empire.[10] In the words of Simon Hornblower, 'the Achaemenid scholarship of the 1980s ... witnessed a kind of anti-colonialist, anti-imperialist reaction comparable to the sloughing-off of "Westerner" mentalities in real-life Iran since 1979'.[11] This feeling of working against a dominant orthodoxy, of their own marginalised status,[12] undoubtedly contributed to a heightened sense of an academic community, and to the energy of the workshops and the publications that emerged from them. At the same time, however, as Hornblower also noted, there was (in those early volumes, and we might add elsewhere) 'an unpleasant note of stridency about some of what was said about the alleged

111

holders of 'traditional views'.[13] The narrative of past scholarship given in many recent accounts has sometimes, it seems,
become ossified into a kind of founding myth – and aspects of
the new narrative of Persian history that has since emerged
have arguably become similarly ossified. Rather as some nineteenth-century writers used the theme of the degeneration of
the Persian monarchy and empire as a kind of default narrative
framework, so there is something similarly automatic about
the way in which 'colourful tales' of court intrigue are now
swiftly classified as part of an 'Orientalist' narrative, and so –
except in so far as they may contain some stray element of
oblique historical interest – put beyond the historian's use.[14]
As we have seen, it is hard – especially in the light of parallels
across history – definitively to exclude the possibility that
stories of court intrigue and violence may have had a significant historical core. (Historical parallels, even in later Iranian
history, suggest that such patterns are all the more likely to
occur in unaccountable monarchies, in which the ruler himself
is vulnerable without the protection of laws.[15])

In parallel to the story of Persian decadence, a new narrative of the resilience of the Persian empire has become
established. Rather than asking why the empire did not last for
longer, or supposing the empire so weak that we rob Alexander of credit for his military victory, we should ask – or so the
story goes – why it lasted as long as it did. The emphasis in
much recent work on the structures and ideologies binding
together the King and his elite, or centre and periphery, or the
new-found evidence of the intensity of bureaucratic control,
certainly discourage the casual view that Persian control was
a passing and superficial one, that Persian administration

merely gave way, or that any setback of the fourth century was the harbinger of inevitable decline and defeat at the hands of Alexander.[16] Though it is questionable perhaps just how widespread such views in fact were,[17] such a concerted approach to the structure and administration of the Persian empire has certainly made these impossible positions for the future. At the same time, however, it is hard to explain the repeated attempts through the fourth century to reclaim the prized imperial possession of Egypt as anything other than a reflection of Persia's *relative* weakness in that period.[18] Legitimate questions can still be asked about the response of the Persian empire to the threat posed by Alexander and the Macedonians.[19] In general, moreover, the depth and detail of a bureaucratic system is rarely an index of the health of the government it serves – bureaucracies, after all, develop their own momentum.[20]

Another question-mark over the Achaemenid Persian empire that refuses to go away is over the degree of impact that it had – both as a model for successor empires, and on its subject peoples. It is at least an open question, as Michel Austin has expressed it crisply, 'whether similarities between Achaemenids and successors arose from similarity of circumstances rather than deliberate imitation'.[21]

As for the impact of empire on the subject peoples, we do not have to revive old clichés of one-way acculturation, or of the feebleness of Persian artistic traditions, to see a problem here. Much recent work has emphasised the open, tolerant, 'systematically cooptive' nature of Persian imperialism,[22] the way, for example, in which the Kings were able to speak to Babylonians or Greeks in their own terms. In the well-chosen words of Haubold, 'the discourse of empire as the Persians conceived it strives to blend into local culture to the point where it divests itself of any obvious sign of Persian authorship'.[23] Put simply, it is hard to combine this emphasis with a strong claim for the Persians' transformation of their empire: the corollary of an 'open' Persian imperialism is that it is likely to have made less mark.

One answer to this might be the matter-of-fact one that the evidence of Persian impact will grow as the archaeological record is expanded.[24] At the same time, however, you would arguably not need to wait for further evidence of the widespread impact of Persian imperialism were it sufficiently obvious. Heleen Sancisi-Weerdenburg put this starkly in summarising the Achaemenid History Workshop's 'two days of intensive discussion' of the theme of centre and periphery: 'one thing has become clear: when one decides to look from the bottom, it is often hard to see the empire'.[25] A more subtle response than merely to wait and see, that of Margaret Cool Root, is to suggest that 'the apparently unimposing impact of Persian culture on the western empire' was itself 'a reflection of the success of the deliberate, assertive central *policy* – as opposed to a vaguely defined tolerant attitude'.[26] The lack of evidence of Persian 'impact' may itself, ironically, testify to impact – albeit of a more insidious, less visible form. 'Control', according to Root, 'focussed on *personal* links of loyalty and cooperation bonding centre and periphery rather than with institutional restructuring and homogenizing.'[27] Though this approach can tip over into a presumption that the very eclecticism of the emerging culture is necessarily a function of Achaemenid presence and ideology, this approach has undoubtedly been a powerful one, responsible for revealing a much more complex, shaded pattern of acculturation in the regions of the empire.[28] At another level, however, this is perhaps merely to rephrase the problem. Personal links may indeed, very effectively, have held the empire together. An imperial ideology seems also to have been widely disseminated, through text and image.[29] The character of Achaemenid imperialism may indeed have allowed for the fostering of new regional cultures (its impact should, of course, also be measured in terms of the interactions *between* subject peoples that it engendered[30]). This is at any rate, however, a very different *kind of impact* from that which other empires have had – as a passing comparison with the Roman empire clearly suggests.[31] As Heleen Sancisi-Weerdenburg herself argued, given the lack of a widely 'shared Persian or Iranian culture' underlying the empire, or given the lack – by comparison with Rome – of a means to propagate a 'verbal and visual ideology',[32] 'it is all the more remarkable that the empire lasted as long as it did':[33] 'In the two centuries of its control, the Persian Empire left its traces, but it did not transform preexisting cultures.' Pierre Briant has indeed gone further, suggesting that the empire's openness to the 'ethnocultural traditions' of its peoples was a central factor in its insufficient resistance to Alexander:[34]

> While there actually was an ideology of the King that continued to function perfectly at the center, an ideology of the Empire did not really exist, even though royal images were spread by means of seals and coins and popular storytellers … In other words, there was no Achaemenid identity that might have induced the peo-

ples, in all of their diversity, to rise up and defend some
common norms.

Another aspect of the new narrative of Persian history that
requires further exploration is its version of Hellenocentrism.
It is an interesting irony that at roughly the point that the
Islamic revolution disrupted Iranian identification with the
pre-Islamic past, and that the (western-led) movement of the
Achaemenid History Workshop set out to reclaim the Achaemenids from an Orientalising, Eurocentric viewpoint, so the
rise of the 'barbarian' began in earnest in classical scholarship.
At least with two of these three trends, this coincidence is not
an accident.[35] The work of Edward Said on 'Orientalism',
which influenced key works on the Greek invention of the
barbarian,[36] was also swiftly taken up by some of the scholars
of the early workshops. Following Said's passing attribution of
the origins of Orientalism to the Greeks,[37] for example, Sancisi-Weerdenburg ascribed to Ctesias the invention of the
category of the 'Oriental' or spoke of how 'the undefined but
implicit "Orientalism" of the fourth-century Greek literature
and the prevalent mental attitudes of Europe-centrism in the
nineteenth century mutually reinforce[d] each other' to create
the version of Persian history against which she and others
were reacting.[38] The work of 'Workshop' scholars is inflected
more broadly with the terminology of 'Orientalism',[39] but at
the same time it is hard to resist the conclusion that the prime
role in the new Achaemenid historiography of Said's work
(and of the exploration of the Greek 'barbarian' that it
spawned) has been to reinforce its founding convictions, to
confirm that the Greeks' accounts of Persia are marked by

pejorative ideas, and so to validate the reversal of Greek stereotypes, rather than to initiate the detailed investigation of Greek attitudes in their own context. Some recent accounts, indeed, seem to reveal a desire to project an outdated view of the Persians onto classical scholars, or to confuse the perspectives of modern scholars with those of the ancient texts they are discussing. 'The old narrative of the Persians as an evil, crude barbarian antithesis to the noble Western (Greek and then Roman) world still runs deep', Root asserts[40] – as if Edith Hall and others were advocating 'Orientalist' views in the classical world, rather than excavating them.

Scholarly accounts of Greek representations of non-Greeks always gave emphasis to the Greeks' own deconstruction of their polarities. As the study of ancient identities and of classical receptions have become almost separate sub-disciplines, however, the barbarian has undeniably become increasingly fragmented, increasingly fluid, and increasingly contested. Recent literature has seen, for example: the attempt (fairly generally) to diminish the currency of the barbarian ideology and to claim that it was purely a manifestation of the Athenian empire; the argument that Herodotean ethnography was driven by disinterested 'scientific' curiosity;[41] or finally the view that luxury borrowings from Persia to Greece (the imitation of Achaemenid metalware in pottery, or the incorporation of items of dress of 'Persian' origin) 'disprove' the old stereotypes of the barbarian.[42] Classicists have also accentuated the differences between authors, salvaging them from a soup of cultural commonplaces and restoring their literary/ideological agency.[43] If a modern critic (Waldemar Januszczak) asks of the burning of Persepolis 'who was the barbarian in that exchange?' he is going no further than Euripides in the context of the Trojan war.[44]

Some of these revisions, of course, are themselves open to question. (They too frequently underestimate the complexity of early accounts of the barbarian.) Though Athenian imperialism may have been a focus for many of the contrasts between Greek and non-Greek, there is reason to suppose, unless you deem Herodotus to have been operating in an exclusively Athenian context, that such ideas had no broader currency. We can be sceptical of the idea of a disinterested scientific curiosity on *a priori* grounds, but this thesis arguably also fails to put the ethnographic sections of Herodotus' *Histories* in the context of Herodotus' work as a whole (in particular, the intense awareness of the relationship of geographical knowledge and power that they evince).[45] As for Greek cultural borrowings from Persia, if items of dress (such as parasols) reserved for the Persian King are adopted in the Greek world by well-to-do Athenian wives, it is evident that such borrowings *need* not contradict, but may actually reinforce, the ideology of Persian effeminacy, say.[46] Contact between peoples does not simply irradiate misunderstanding. (And whatever 'smattering of Persian' Greeks may have had 'would hardly have provided [them] with an open-sesame into Persian culture'.[47]) The relationship of Greek to Near Eastern cultures (like that of any different cultures) presented a complex mix: of awe and resentment, of real engagement and wilful garbling.[48]

It would be wrong to give the impression equally that 'Classics' is now a discipline entirely at ease with a new more equal relationship with neighbouring ancient (and later) civilisations. (It is hard, for example, to suppress the suspicion that lying behind the backlash against the Greek-barbarian polarity – reminiscent of some of the anti-anti-imperialist backlash against Said and Orientalism – there lies an unwillingness to 'taint' classical authors by ascribing to them chauvinistic attitudes.) In some respects, however, the recent study of the barbarian has now left the new Achaemenid historiography high and dry. In particular, an increasing pattern is to give agency to those caricatured within Greek texts, to suggest – on the model of an excellent study of Herodotus' use of Egyptian sources[49] – that Greek material on Persia likewise may include much that is valuable of contemporary Persian cultural representations, not only nuggets of Persian fact.[50] One recent suggestion, for example, is that the invention of the barbarian may have been a discourse to which the Persian King himself contributed, one 'sparked by Persian attempts to fashion a cultural language that would speak to both ruler and ruled'.[51] The theme of the Persian King's decadence, it has been suggested, has its origins likewise in a Persian discourse (the blackening of Artaxerxes II by his brother Cyrus) and was never perhaps so pronounced or straightforward as it may have seemed.[52] All this has uncomfortable implications for the new Achaemenid historiography in so far as it destabilises the clean distinction between Greek and Persian sources on which much recent work depends. Artefacts, it seems, can defy ethnic classification but texts cannot.[53] At the same time, the relentless positivist drive of much recent Achaemenid historiography[54] – together with its focus on structures, and its reliance on the Greeks' 'distancing' of the Near Eastern as a founding charter for revisionism –

have all tended to reduce the significance of Greek representations: to cast them as the chaff, rather than the substance,
of Persian history. (Ironically Briant's recent treatment of
Darius III has itself been trenchantly criticised by an Achaemenid colleague for 'reduc[ing] history to a literary and
rhetorical exercise rather than a discipline'.[55]) The judgements
drawn on Persian women by Greek writers 'do not further our
understanding of the functioning of the Achaemenid empire'.[56] Persian foreign policy, or political thought, should be
reconstructed from limited Persian material rather than by
credulous reliance on Greek sources.[57]

Unquestionably, you cannot hope to access Persian foreign
policy, as if from a leader's keynote address, from the pages of
Herodotus' *Histories*. The pattern in Greek sources, for example, whereby the Persian Kings are represented as striving for
world domination indeed cannot simply be read off the page
as a realistic description of Darius' or Xerxes' 'war goals'.[58]
Greek sources may nonetheless contain (in complexly altered
form) the echoes of Persian rhetoric, Persian ideology (and in
so doing, of course, add to the evidence of the ideological
impact of Persian imperialism). Herodotus' focus on revenge,
for example, as a motive for the Persians' expedition against
Greece is generally given short shrift.[59] However, the emphasis on the King's 'helping his friends and harming his enemies'
– to use a Greek phrase – is so strong a pattern in the Persian
royal inscriptions as to make such a focus on vengeance at least
readily comprehensible. 'Within these countries, the man who
was loyal, him I rewarded well; (him) who was evil, him I
punished well ....'[60] The King does not want to have to punish
injustice, but that is just the way it is. 'It is not my desire that

a man should do harm; nor indeed is that my desire, if he should do harm, he should not be punished.'[61] The same binary approach to reward and punishment is reflected in a number of episodes within the *Histories*, for example in the Persian threats passed on by the Ionian tyrants on the eve of the battle of Lade (the concluding act of the Ionian revolt[62]):

'Promise that, if they abandon their allies, there will be no disagreeable consequences for them; we will not set fire to their houses or their temples, or treat them with any greater harshness than before this trouble occurred. If, however, they refuse, and insist upon open fighting, then you must resort to threats, and say exactly what we will do to them: tell them, that is, that when they are beaten they will be sold as slaves, that their boys will be made eunuchs, their girls carried off to Bactria, and their land given to others.'

A new phase of Persian historiography, then, might benefit from a stronger focus on cultural representations, from a fuller, more sympathetic engagement with Greek material – and arguably a more cautious, more philosophical position vis-à-vis the possibility of historical reconstruction. 'Confronted by a text without "facts"', as Heleen Sancisi-Weerdenburg put it, 'our first inclination is to think that they are omitted, but – as we hope or expect – that they should be there, hidden behind sentences of an abstract nature.'[63] This sentiment, originally in the context of the Persian royal inscriptions, arguably applies more broadly: this account has been awash with claims to represent another's viewpoint (so much so that one is tempted to despair at this perennial failure of communication): the claim of Greek writers or British imperialists to ventriloquise the Persian; the claim for Persian art that it represents the points of view of Persia's subjects, and many more. It has also seen repeated scepticism over those claims, the tendency to seek to distinguish between the authentic and the inauthentic voice. Self-evidently, however, the experience of any empire is made up of the voices of both rulers and subjects. If we are not tacitly to be impelled by Persian imperial ideology, to be drawn in by the 'magnetic force of [its] imperial centredness',[64] to identify disproportionately with the imperial project, Greek representations (and *others*) need to be embraced as evidence in their own right, not only for a kind of ideological clearing exercise before the real work of historical extraction begins.[65]

There is perhaps a bigger problem lurking here, however, which needs to be overcome – and that is the assumption of continuity in ancient attitudes to the 'Orient' from the ancient world to the present day. This is arguably a problem common both to Persian historians and to classicists, to the original proponents of a Greek-barbarian polarity and to the representatives of the backlash against it. When in a recent collection of essays, it was announced that the Persian wars were 'a defining moment in the history of the world',[66] this was not so much a hard-nosed historical judgement of its consequences as an assessment based primarily on *others*' assessments across history: the Persian wars have become defining in so far as so many people have seen them as such. For others, however (such as Victor Davis Hanson, in reviewing the same collection), this is not a matter of representation but of reality (of course this distinction is over-harsh): 'such a clash of disparate civilisations ... for centuries has been emblematic of many of the differences we still undeniably see today between the East and the West'.[67] An aura of inevitability hangs over the clash of East and West, a sense that has understandably grown since the attack on the World Trade Center of 11 September 2001.

Of course, there have been attempts to up-end the tidy analogy of ancient and modern, at least rhetorically. Neil McGregor's analogy of the alliance of George Bush, Tony Blair and other western leaders against Saddam Hussein and the Athenians' alliance against Persia, if it is more than a glib parallel, in fact interestingly turns the usual power-dynamic of ancient Orientalism on its head, suggesting that both contrived to maintain a negative (implicitly, false) image of Persia for domestic purposes. In the same way, Tom Holland in his *Persian Fire* (the publication of which coincided happily with the exhibition), reversed expectations, on his jacket blurb, by equating the Persian empire with Bush's America, 'a global superpower ... determined to bring truth and order to ... two terrorist states', Athens and Sparta, 'eccentric cities in a poor and mountainous backwater'.[68] But these reversals, partly perhaps because they are predicated on such a deeply rooted sense of a historical pattern, seem not in any way to shift perceptions. At times, there seems almost a wilful desire to exploit the assumption of continuity. Anthony Pagden, for example, in his recent book *Worlds at War*, pays due attention to many differences in context, and yet latches onto even superficial resemblances between ancient and modern to construct a narrative of the, seemingly inevitable, chasm between

East and West. The casual tale of the genesis of his book is perhaps the best illustration:[69]

> One morning, over breakfast my wife, the classical scholar Giulia Sissa, was looking at a picture in the *New York Times* of a group of Iranians prostrate in prayer. 'How ironic!', she remarked. 'It was just this habit of prostration which most horrified the Greeks about the ancient Persians'. And she added: 'perhaps there is something here you could write a book about'.

We need to be very clear then in our emphasis on the historical discontinuities and differences of context between ancient and modern 'Orientalism'.[70] First, without our necessarily subscribing to the patriotic myth of the Greeks as heroic underdogs, it is beyond doubt that, up to the conquests of Alexander, the relationship of Greeks and Persians was one in which the military-political boot was on the *Persian* foot. In some ways indeed there is a defensive or reactive quality to Greek chauvinism, evident for example in their mocking naming of pyramids after their own cheesecakes and crocodiles after lizards and so on, or in the pathetic claims of fringe courtiers in Herodotus' *Histories* to be close to the Persian King.[71] Secondly, the Greeks were by no means unique in their chauvinistic attitudes to other cultures. What Herodotus claims of the Persians, that they considered themselves the most virtuous, their neighbours the next most virtuous and so on, seems to be borne out by Persian sources for royal ideology.[72] Similarly (as Herodotus was again well aware), the Egyptians were profoundly resistant to foreign cultures, mirroring for example the linguistic ethnocentrism of the Greeks – calling any who did not speak the same language 'barbarian'.[73]

Unless we subscribe to Hanson's hypothesis of a superior 'Western way of war', moreover, there was nothing inevitable about either of the major Greek victories over the Persians. Though Alexander's conquest may in part have been fed (and in a sense have fulfilled) earlier Greek representations of eastern barbarians,[74] 'Persia was not a dead duck on the day that Alexander began his campaign'.[75] Likewise, as Herodotus saw only too clearly, if the Persians had avoided any one of a number of wrong turnings, if they had stooped to bribing the leading figures of the Greek cities, or if Themistocles had been more scrupulous in handling his fellow Greek commanders, the outcome may well have been different.[76] What difference would this have made? If, as a fundamental modern view has it, it was the jostle and thrust of polis debate, of face-to-face society, that engendered the best aspects of Greek culture and thought,[77] then Persian victory might have cut off the life-blood of Greek civilisation. 'Had Xerxes succeeded', according to Pagden,[78]

> … there would have been no Greek theatre, no Greek science, no Plato, no Aristotle, no Sophocles nor Aeschylus. That incredible burst of creative energy which took place during the fifth and fourth centuries BCE and which laid the foundation for all later Western civilisation, would never have happened.

'If you want proof of the deadening effect of Persian rule,

according to Hanson again, 'why not simply compare pre-Persian Ionia , home of the birth of the Greek renaissance in epic, lyric and presocratic philosophy, with its subsequent intellectual life in the sixth and fifth centuries as a Persian satrapy?'[79] But this is almost certainly vastly exaggerated. It is very likely that the Persian King would not have bothered much with the political systems in place in the Greek cities, so long as they did not cause trouble – the aftermath of the Ionian revolt saw the Persians deposing the tyrants of some Greek cities and introducing democracy in their place.[80] And it is questionable whether for the vast majority of (very small) cities in the Greek world, whose power of action was in any event vastly circumscribed and who operated in the shadow of their larger neighbours, a change in the background power would have made very much difference.[81] In the King's self-image as a global policeman, and in the related characterisation of the Greeks as held back by their petty squabbles, it is possible to glimpse indeed how Medism might have seemed not only an acceptable but even an *idealistic* option to some Greeks.[82] It is impossible to say whether a *Pax Persica* – and an accompanying abatement of inter-polis rivalry or, alternatively, a wave of cultural resistance – might not actually have enhanced Greek creativity rather than annihilating it.

If classical scholarship is still in some senses imprisoned by the *original* status of the Greeks, and by the assumption of an East-West division, the same is perhaps scarcely less true of modern scholarship on Persia – founded as it was on the polarity of Greek and Barbarian. In the splendid ending to his *Sparta and Persia*, David Lewis digressed in Herodotean fashion to cover the history of tension between Greece and Turkey over the islands of the Aegean. After expressing his cynicism over the hope of a negotiated solution ('the study of history does not always encourage a belief in human reason') he concludes: 'we should not think our story is yet at an end'.[83] The hope may be premature, but is no less worth expressing: that the Persian wars, or at least their proxy scholarly conflict, might be drawn to some kind of conclusion.

Notes

Preface

1. For a narrative of Sykes' career, see Wynn 2003.

2. Though see e.g. Roaf 1998 for an argument that the Sassanians associated Persepolis with legendary heroes such as Jamshid rather than the Achaemenids.

3. See Kuhrt 1983 for a robust placing of the Cylinder in its Babylonian context. Recent examples of the elevation of the Cyrus Cylinder include those of Shirin Ebadi (Nobel Lecture, Oslo, 10 Dec. 2003, calling it 'one of the most important documents that should be studied in the history of human rights') and George W. Bush (in his Commencement Address at the US Merchant Marine Academy, 19 June 2006). For a recent popular rebuttal of these claims, see Matthias Schulz, 'Falling for ancient propaganda', *Spiegel*, available at http://www.spiegel.de/international/world/0,1518,566027,00.html – accessed 9/1/2010.

4. Notwithstanding Briant's insistence, 2002: 77, that 'neither Cyrus nor Cambyses had the simple aim of ruling in name only over some sort of loose federation'. See here Tuplin's 1987 survey of Achaemenid administration, concluding (p. 158, citing Cook 1983: 173) that 'the proposition that "there was no uniform infrastructure of Achaemenid rule ..." may be destined to stand (it may even be the simple truth)', and the observations of Briant 2002: 447-8.

5. For a full English text, with notes and further references, see Kuhrt 2007: 70-4. For the significance of the title King of Anshan, see Henkelman 2008: 55-7 (countering Potts 2005, who argues for a distinctly Anshanite character to Cyrus and his ancestors; cf. also Waters 2004).

6. For Darius' accession, see esp. Herodotus 3.67-88 and the various versions of the Behistun inscription (DB), for which see Kuhrt 2007: 141-58.

7. See further below, Chapter 1.

8. CMa; cf. CMb, CMc, with Waters 1996, Stronach 1997b.

9. Stronach 1997a: 50 (contrast Jacobs 2010); Stronach 1997b: 361-2

postulates 'division and rapprochement' between the Behistun inscription and the interventions by Darius at Pasargadae.

10. 'Alexander, no doubt reluctantly, lit the funeral pyre of the Hellenic crusade' (Badian 1985: 447). For the destruction of Persepolis as a fulfilment of a Panhellenic promise, see esp. Flower 2000: esp. 113-15; for burning as the outcome of a failure of policy of conciliation, Briant 1980: 81-3, Nawotka 2003; cf. Sancisi-Weerdenburg 1993a, emphasising Alexander's destruction of Persepolis as a source of power-relationships, Fredricksmeyer 2000: 147-50 emphasising the religious status of Persepolis, Badian 1985: 443-7, connecting it to uncertainty over events in Greece. Badian 1985: 445 'the burning was an act of policy'.

11. A phrase of Briant's which goes back at least as far as the conclusion of 1979a (p. 1414); see also e.g. Briant 2002: 2, and cf. Frye 1983: 135 (describing Alexander likewise as 'perhaps the real heir of the Achaemenids'); for Alexander's use of Persian royal ideology see e.g. Briant 1980, Harrison 2009. See Lane Fox 2007, Wiemer 2007, for a critique of the phrase 'last of the Achaemenids'; cf. Tuplin 2008: 109 for a balanced judgement.

12. As Briant puts it eloquently in his 'ego-histoire', 2002: 2, 'what came before Alexander was never defined except as a foil to what came after'. See Briant 1979a for a fascinating statement of the origins of his thinking.

13. In the fine phrase of Briant 1979a: 1378. For this emphasis on continuity see e.g. Sancisi-Weerdenburg, Kuhrt and Root 1994, and most recently Briant and Joannès 2006; for some, more recent reaction, see below, Chapter 6.

14. See esp. now Henkelman 2008 (for a general formulation, p. 8); Cameron 1936 is notable for concluding its history of early Iran with the arrival of Cyrus the Great.

15. See below, Chapter 5.

16. For an account of the genesis of the workshops, see Kuhrt 2009.

17. The phrase of Nylander 1993: 145-6; see also Stolper 1999: 1112, on how until recently 'les historiens modernes du Proche-Orient ont travaillé sous l'influence de leur formation classique'.

18. Sancisi-Weerdenburg 1990a: 254.

19. As Christopher Tuplin suggests to me, 'the Workshop was setting out to put a shape on a process of study already in train'. Cf. Briant 1979a, characterising the approach to Achaemenid history of the last fifteen years as having been revitalised. See further below, Chapter 5.

20. Sancisi-Weerdenburg 1990a: 257 acknowledging that the 'search for the structure of the Achaemenid Empire is, of course, not confined to the papers submitted to these annual meetings' (referencing Briant's collection *Rois, Tribut, Paysans*, 1982).

21. Sancisi-Weerdenburg 1984: 187; cf. Briant 1982: 506, 1988: 138n.2.

22. Briant 2002: 3, originally published in French in 1996; cf. Briant 2001.

23. Sancisi-Weerdenburg 1990a: 257.

24. The *Bulletin d'Histoire Achéménide*, under Briant's aegis, is organised, moreover, in such a way as to follow his history's thematic structure (Briant 2002: xv). See also Weber and Wiesehöfer's 1996 bibliography.

25. Briant 2002: 5. See also Briant 2003a: 12 for the claim ('impression evidemment fugitive', as he says himself) to have exhausted the possibilities of the structural analysis of the Persian empire.

26. Briant 2002: 13-14, including the statement that 'Persian history ... was never treated in antiquity by a historian of the stature of a Polybius'.

27. See e.g. the excellent accounts of Hallock 1971, D.M. Lewis 1990 and 1994, and (for the fullest and most up-to-date account) Henkelman 2008: 65-179; for the size of the archive see also Jones and Stolper 2008. For the archive as stored rather than discarded, see Henkelman 2008: 70-1, 162-71, Brosius 2003c: 264-5.

28. For this story, embracing extraordinary publications such as Cameron 1948, Hallock 1969, see Henkelman 2008: 65-179; Cameron 1948: vii-x gives a vivid illustration of the practical difficulties. There are doubtless other parallel developments worth exploring, not least the *Transeuphratène* group, and ongoing linguistic scholarship (sometimes at odds with the work of historians: Kellens 1992: 420).

29. See e.g. Sancisi-Weerdenburg 1987d: 490 (in the context of a review of Cook 1983) on the attempt to see the Persian empire as 'a complex and intricate pattern of political, social, economic and cultural interaction between the King, the administrative institutions of the various levels and the subject populations'. Sancisi-Weerdenburg describes the emphasis on structures as a means of evading Hellenocentric stereotypes, 1987a: xiii.

30. See esp. Kuhrt 2007: chs 15-16 for a selection of texts.

31. Sancisi-Weerdenburg 1987c: 131.

32. See e.g. Sancisi-Weerdenburg 1984: 185: 'when Alexander arrived he had to deal merely the final blow to an empire which had mostly succumbed to endemic diseases: corruption, harem intrigues, weak kings, to name but a few'.

33. I hesitate to describe it as revisionist – for me a term with no necessarily negative connotations – in the light of Amélie Kuhrt's withering response to the term at the 2005 conference on the 'World of the Achaemenids' (published as Kuhrt 2010); cf. Lane Fox 2007: 268.

34. And indeed to exceed them: see esp. the presentation of the Cyrus Cylinder and of the Achaemenids' alleged policy of religious tolerance in the video accompanying the exhibition, *Persepolis Recreated* (contrast Kuhrt 1983); see further the museum catalogue, Curtis and Tallis 2005.

35. In a common phrase of Briant's (cf. Stolper 1999: 1124): 'décryptage'; see also the metaphor of 'cleansing', e.g. Briant 2002: 762. Contrast Briant's formula (2002: 8), 'however partisan and ideological a Greek text

may be, when it is located within the web of its associations, it can provide a stimulating Achaemenid reading'.

1. Against the Grain

1. In the much-quoted phrase of Iris Murdoch (*The Nice and the Good* (London, 1968) 171) 'it is a game with very few pieces where the skill of the player lies in complicating the rules. The isolated and uneloquent fact must be exhibited within a tissue of hypothesis subtle enough to let it speak'.

2. Cf. Armayor 1978, emphasising the Greek-centred view of catalogues, D.M. Lewis 1985: esp. 116-17; for the relationship of Herodotus' account and Behistun, see Martorelli 1977, West 2007, and esp. the balanced conclusion of Asheri 1999: 116.

3. Contrast DSe 30-34; cf. DNa 32, DNb 16-21 with Herodotus 5.49, 7.9.b1-2.

4. Briant 1989a.

5. For 'deformation', see Murray 1987.

6. Cf. Bovon 1963 for the portrayal of Persian warriors in Greek art, or the observations of Tuplin 1996: 136 ('a thoroughly assimilated stereotype which did not need to carry many ethnographically precise markers').

7. See Harrison 2000: 45-8 for one attempt to navigate these problems.

8. Tuplin 1990: esp. 21, 28; for *Cyropaedia*, see also esp. Gera 1993, Sancisi-Weerdenburg 1987c, 1985. Ctesias is usually deemed to have reaped little advantage from his spell in the court of Artaxerxes (Sancisi-Weerdenburg 1987b, Bigwood 1978), although for a compelling reappraisal of the nature of his works, see e.g. Lenfant 2001: 433-8, 2004, Stronk 2007, Llewellyn-Jones and Robson 2010; on his medical background, Tuplin 2004. For other fourth-century *Persica*, see Stevenson 1987, 1997 and esp. now Lenfant 2009.

9. D.M. Lewis 1994: 20 ('I used to say that its strangeness could be encapsulated in the fact that it formed its plurals in -p, until I said it once too often at a dinner party and was told firmly that Georgian did so too'); for a recent summary of the problems, see Kuhrt 2007: 763-70.

10. Henkelman 2008: 79, 177-9; for possible missing classes of material, pp. 83-5, Hallock 1973: 322-3.

11. Root 1979, Nylander 1970.

12. See Chapter 4 below for discussion of the 'daiva' inscription. Cf. Briant 2002: 8: 'the royal inscriptions truly mirror the vision the Great Kings had of their power, their virtues, and their imperial reach'.

13. For explorations, see e.g. Wiesehöfer 1978, Balcer 1987; for the reliefs, see Root 1979: ch. 5. Contrast Briant 2002: 114: 'Once the propagandistic distortions of the new king have been carefully bracketed [!], his version is far more useful than Herodotus's'.

14. Tuplin 2005: 235; contrast Sancisi-Weerdenburg 1999 on Behistun as 'history' (and on the non-historical focus of Persian royal inscriptions in

general), hypothesising royal letters as a source for the text (pp. 103-4). Cf. Momigliano 1975: 126: 'Perhaps the three elements of Persian education – to ride a horse, to shoot straight and to tell the truth – were not favourable to the formation of a historian'.

15. Herodotus 7.136, 1.134; for *proskynesis* see e.g. Bickermann 1963, Briant 2002: 222-3, Wiesehofer 2003.

16. Amory 1929: 68, 61. Cf. Curzon 1892: ii.195, cited by Roaf 1990: 105 ('It is all the same and the same again, and yet again ...'); Mortimer Wheeler 1968: 56, 58, cited by Root 1990: 121 ('these mournful, immobile processions ... have about them a semblance of the pageantry of death'). Boardman revives this negative view of the Persepolis reliefs, e.g. 2000: 126-7.

17. Roaf 1983, 1990.

18. 1979: 311.

19. Root 1990: 121: 'These delegates bring not only themselves, but also the accumulated wealth of re-established wholeness.'

20. Root 1979: 311.

21. Briant 2002: 8:

22. Allen 2005a: 100.

23. Sancisi-Weerdenburg 1993b: 146, citing Momigliano 1975: 142; Briant 2002: 7. See also Sancisi-Weerdenburg 1983: 21 (Herodotus' Persians 'are far less stereotyped than those of later generations of Greek writers'), 23 (on his 'honest guidance').

24. Allen 2005a: 10, 56, 11, 83. Boardman perhaps exaggerates in suggesting that Herodotus 'is often neglected or disparaged now for being "Greek"', 2000: 14.

25. Briant 2002: 9.

26. E.g. Briant 2002: 112 (though contrast p. 235).

27. Briant 2002: 7.

28. See e.g. Redfield 1985, Hartog 1988, Hall 1989, Thomas 2000, Munson 2001; see further Chapter 6 below. Cf. Sancisi-Weerdenburg 1987b: 43-4, crediting Ctesias with the invention of the Orient, and her generally laudatory review of Hall's influential *Inventing the Barbarian*, 1993c (though pointing out a plethora of mistakes on Persian context), latching on to the way in which the 'barbarian' undermines the factuality of Greek sources for Persian history.

29. Briant 2002: 7; for the end of the *Histories* see esp. Boedeker 1988, Dewald 1997, Desmond 2004.

30. Briant 1982: 494-5; cf. D.M. Lewis 1985 for a more sceptical approach.

31. E.g. Briant 2002: 158: 'as usual, *Herodotus* brings his bias to the historical reconstruction'.

32. 2002: 142-3; cf. Briant's bald summary of the limitations of fourth-century historians, 2002: 612.

33. Briant 2002: 130-40. Cf. Allen 2005a: 47: 'Herodotus' highly

personalized account attributes the entire affair to one Aristagoras, the ruler of Miletus' (Ionian revolt). Cf. D.M. Lewis 1977: 25-6 for an argument that personal grudges in fact influenced the Persian kings.

34. Rood 1998: ch. 10.

35. Briant 2002: 149.

36. Harrison 2003a, responding to Forrest 1979 (cf. Harrison 2002 for accumulation of causes). Contrast Sancisi-Weerdenburg 1983: 27, for whom the personal anecdotes of the Greek historians merely fill in for the lack of 'real knowledge of the general social and cultural background of the Persians'; cf. Cawkwell 2005: 62.

37. Hdt 3.125, 129-37, with Griffiths 1987, arguing that Democedes is in large part a 'folk-tale hero'.

38. See e.g. Histiaeus of Miletus: Herodotus 5.23-4, 35-6, 106-7.

39. Herodotus 3.137: Democedes passed on that he was engaged to the daughter of the wrestler, Milo – this was to prove that he was an important person in his own home.

40. Briant 2002: 139; 'it is hard to separate history from fairy tale in Herodotus's story'.

41. For the question of the extent to which the pattern of personal relationships between King and Greek cities was intentionally fostered, see Austin 1990, esp. 298-306, emphasising also the role of Greek initiative.

42. See e.g. Harrison 2003a; for Syloson, van der Veen 1996, for patterns of contingency Irwin and Greenwood 2007: 36-8.

43. 2002: 8 (my italics). Cf. Briant's self-defence, 2009a: 144n.14, against the charges of dismissing Greek sources on Persia (laid by Garvin 2003: 89n.11 and Brosius 2006b). His approach is 'rather more complex and elaborate ...: it is not about simplistically reasoning by exclusives (yes/no), but about understanding that the literary Classical tradition is at the same time useful and deforming'.

44. Cf. West 2003: 437 ('These tales should not be treated as precious nuggets of Persian history thinly overlaid with a Greek veneer'), Kuhrt 2003: 357 on the stories of Cyrus' and Sargon's (and 'the futility of attempts to disinter a "nugget" of historical truth from such tales'). Sancisi-Weerdenburg employs a different analogy, of the 'unlocking' of Achaemenid evidence from the *Cyropaedia*, 1987c: 35: 'At present the main problem is which key to use in order to unlock this chest.'

45. See Sancisi-Weerdenburg 1988b, 1994b for arguments that the Median empire was, to a significant extent (she does not dispute that there may have been some 'developments of a state-formation kind') a (Greek or Persian) fiction; see further Lanfranchi, Roaf and Rollinger 2003, Waters 2010 (and Roaf 2010) for a corrective. Katouzian 2009: 29-30 provides a salutary reminder of the dangers of a literal approach to the sources.

46. Briant 2002: 26. Cf. Sancisi-Weerdenburg 1994b: 55 ('a typical description of an ordinary Greek tyrant's rise to power', although reflecting Achaemenid court practice).

47. Fehling 1989; for a violent reaction to Fehling and the 'Liar School' see Pritchett 1993, and for a nuanced middle path, Moles 1993. Contrast Sancisi-Weerdenburg 1994b: 43, arguing on the basis of the story's plausibility ('Historians do not tend to write implausible histories') that the logos was 'primarily a Greek product', though drawing on Babylonian traditions.

48. Sancisi-Weerdenburg 1987b: 34.

49. For the latter, see Sancisi-Weerdenburg 1994b. Sancisi-Weerdenburg argues against the orality of the Median logos, on the grounds that oral traditions tend to concern 'faits et gestes', rather than following a chronological framework. As she acknowledges, however, the story of Deioces does concern concrete actions (and indeed, it might be said to put an exaggerated focus on Deioces' cunning as a factor in the development of monarchy). The fact that the story also contains abstract terminology and value judgements does not seem to me to constitute an argument against the orality of this part of the Median logos. See also now Panaino 2003, Meier et al. (2004), examining the logos from multiple perspectives, Munson 2009: 459-62 (arguing for 'Median' elements in the Median logos); Steiner 1994: 128-32 for the association of tyranny and writing.

50. In the broader Aesopian sense of 'moral': Harrison 2000: 242 in the context of Herodotus' judgement on the Athenians' participation in the Ionian revolt (5.97.3). For the relationship of orality with moral shaping of logoi, see Murray 1987.

51. Herodotus 2.151-3; for an Egyptian narrative context for the story see Dillery 2005.

52. Contrast Sancisi-Weerdenburg 1993b: 146 (cf. 1994b: 55) focussing on the story of Deioces as a 'Greek tyrant's progress' – though one with 'unmistakable Iranian elements ... recognisable'. See also Kurke 1999: ch. 2 for a nuanced exploration of Herodotus' presentation of Greek and Persian tyranny in the *Histories*, Harrison 2003b for the quasi-philosophical exploration of Egyptian kingship.

53. See e.g. Hartog 1988, Boedeker 1988.

54. See e.g. the observations of West 2003; cf. Murray 1987: 114-15.

55. Both these examples relate to Peisistratus' seizure of the Athenian tyranny, Herodotus 1.59-64. Andrewes 1956 might be taken as emblematic of a more confident, traditional approach to such source problems in archaic history. Ironically, the evidence for the Peisistratid tyranny was a focus also of Sancisi-Weerdenburg 2000.

56. Sourvinou-Inwood 1991: 191-284. Cf. Briant 2002: 31 on 'factual elements in the founder legends'. It is noteworthy that Briant eschews the hunt for the 'noyau informatif' in his later study of Darius III, Briant 2003a: 18.

57. For one alternative reading of the Phye/Peisistratus episode, see e.g. Connor 1987.

58. Lenfant 2007: 55

59. See e.g. Briant 2002: 369 on smuggled messages.

60. Briant 2002: 91; cf. pp. 131-2 for the story of Intaphernes' intrusion on Darius as evidence that the King was 'not totally sure of his power', and that the initial privileges of access of the fellow-conspirators were soon revoked. Contrast the nuanced treatment of the Intaphernes story, and of its relationship to the preceding chapter, of Griffiths 2001: 174-8.

61. Briant 1979a: 1388.

62. Allen 2005a: 97 (cf. p. 57), characterising Greek accounts of the Persian court as 'simplified and glamorous morality tales ... rather than factual accounts'.

2. The Persian Version

1. Hecataeus 1 F 1; for Cerberus F 27; for Hecataeus' (and his contemporaries') historical methods, see esp. R. Fowler 1996, for 'demythologisation' West 2002.

2. Contrast the focus of Stolper 1999, not on reconstructing the Persian 'point of view' but on a Near Eastern context for Persian history.

3. See below, Chapter 6, for a more complex pattern.

4. Or so I was told, as an incoming graduate student in 1990, during an exhaustive, shelf-by-shelf tour of the library.

5. Allen 2005a: 177.

6. Kent 1953: DSf.

7. Cook 1962: 126, cited by Root 1979: 11 (repeated by Cook 1983: 163-4, though concluding that 'it is still largely a matter of subjective judgement'); for Telephanes see Pliny, *Natural History* 34, 19.68. Kawami 1986: 264, 267 goes further in attributing specific works to Telephanes; see, however, Root's critique, 1990: 133.

8. Richter 1949: 176, followed by e.g. Boardman 1964: 118-25. For a critique of this trend, see Gates 2003: 110-11; for a discussion of how widespread such ideas were, see Chapter 5 below.

9. Richter 1949: 180; cf. an anonymous German textbook, cited by Wiesehöfer 1996: 86.

10. Richter 1946: 27, 1949: 179; cf. Frankfort 1946: 12, Richter 1949: 176 for Lycian art.

11. See esp. Stronach 1978: 39-43; cf. also Boardman 2000: 53-60.

12. Berenson 1954: 186 (cited by Nylander 1970: 148).

13. Root 1979; cf. more restrainedly Stronach 1978: 'the oft-cited eclecticism of Achaemenian art and architecture bore a political dimension'. See also now Razmjou 2010 for an emphasis on the symbolic role of the Persepolis treasury, 'an early kind of museum' (p. 243).

14. Root 1990: 118-19. See also now Gopnik 2010 for the (compelling) thesis of the multi-rowed hall of columns as an expression of unity in diversity.

15. Sancisi-Weerdenburg 1993b: 154.

16. See, however, Stronach 1997a for the 'visible divide between the imagery of Cyrus and Darius' (p. 40).

17. For a defence against the proposition that this is art built by assembly line, see Root 1990: 128: 'somewhere between patron and sculptural piecework, a significant role was played by artists of great talent'.

18. The phrase is Root's, 1991: 9; cf. Gunter 1990: esp. 135.

19. E.g. Dusinberre 2003: 29, 171.

20. Briant 2001, and for a gazetteer of new archaeological research across the empire Briant and Boucharlat 2005. Contrast Boardman 2000: 224, and see further below, Chapter 6.

21. Allen 2005a: 177.

22. Though contrast e.g. Victor Davis Hanson, e.g. 2007, and many of the popular responses to the *Forgotten Empire* exhibition discussed below, Chapter 6.

23. Cf. Sancisi-Weerdenburg 1983: 31: 'The real downfall did not take place until 150 years after Salamis and that is rather a retarded effect.'

24. 'We should not assume that paperwork was always immaculate': D.M. Lewis 1990: 5; cf. D.M. Lewis 1977: 25-6, on e.g. the story in *Ezra* of the wide search for a lost document, *Ezra* V17-VI2. For a full account of the administration of the Persepolis fortification archive, see Henkelman 2008: 136-62.

25. E.g. Sancisi-Weerdenburg 1987d: 492-3, criticising Cook 1983.

26. 'Bâtisseurs de l'empire', in the title of the section heading of Briant's history. Cf. Brosius 2006a: 13 for a (very telegraphic) account of Cambyses' reign without any sign of controversy: 'During his reign Cyprus came under Persian control and in 525 he conquered Egypt. Cambyses was proclaimed pharaoh and was given the name Mesuti-Re, "Son of (the god) Re".'

27. Sancisi-Weerdenburg 1995a: 1048; Brosius 2006a: 24 (cf. Briant 2002: 529) on 'Persian success' at Thermopylae.

28. Allen 2005a: 35. Cf. Brosius' reconstruction, 2006a: 9, of the 'obscure' motives of Astyages for attacking Cyrus ('It may have been due to his ambition to expand the Median realm, but he could also have recognised the growing power of Cyrus and was compelled to react before his power could pose a political threat'), Young 1980: 219 on the 'natural thrust of [Persian] expansion'.

29. Briant 2002: 51. Cf. Cruz-Uribe's plausible reconstruction of the logistics of the campaign, 2003: 20-6.

30. Razmjou 2002: 94.

31. Lecoq 1997: DSab, with Kuhrt 2007: 477-82; cf. Root 1979: 144-7 for the (contrasting) dignified portrayal of the King's subjects. See further below, ch. 4.

32. Herodotus 3.1-3; cf. Ctesias 688 F 13a, and for this pattern of 'genealogical parasitism', Sancisi-Weerdenburg 1994b: 53, and esp. Tuplin 1991: 256-9.

33. See now Dillery 2005 for an exploration of these traditions in an

Egyptian narrative context, Lang 1972 on Nitetis as one 'stubborn fact' in the story. Cf. Briant 2002: 49, 51 for a greater focus on Persian propaganda, Griffiths 1989 for comparison of traditions concerning Cambyses and the Spartan Cleomenes.

34. D.M. Lewis 1977: 25-6 offers some possible instances.

35. See Sancisi-Weerdenburg's critique (1987d: 490) of J.M. Cook's 'basic weakness' in his 1983 history of the Persian empire, 'an inclination to bridge gaps in the evidence and to fill in blanks in our knowledge of the Persian empire by speculative description'.

36. Brosius 2006a: 24 ('In the eyes of Xerxes the Persian objective of the campaign, the punishment of Athens had been achieved' – by her occupation).

37. Herodotus 5.97.

38. Herodotus 5.102.

39. Parker 1983: 168n.133.

40. Kuhrt 1995: 667.

41. Allen 2005a: 47

42. Mistakenly in my view: the emphasis is amoral (see Harrison 2000: 242).

43. For Herodotus' account of the Ionian revolt Murray 1988, and (from a different perspective) Georges 2000; cf. Cawkwell 2005: ch. 4, representing Aristagoras a 'man of political vision' and 'one of the heroes of Greek liberty' (p. 76). Briant, strikingly, interprets Herodotus' account (e.g. Dionysius of Phocaea's speech, and the Ionians' response, at 6.11-12) literally: 'The fighting spirit that the commander Dionysius tried to instil in his troops rapidly faded, with the soldiers refusing to undergo the difficult discipline he tried to impose on them', Briant 2002: 155; 'The plaints put in the soldiers' mouths ... evidence deep discouragement', 2002: 156. The episode should be interpreted as a dramatic illustration, written of course in knowledge of the outcome, of the Ionians' fractiousness and unreadiness for revolt.

44. Contrast Brosius 2006a: 22: 'An accidental fire destroyed the entire city, including the temple of Cybele.'

45. Kuhrt 1995: 671; she then proceeds to discuss the League's triumphs.

46. Balcer 1989: 130, 137, 140.

47. Balcer 1989, 1995; see also Young 1980, mainly focussing on the size of the Persian army and questions of logistics.

48. Kuhrt 1995: 670-1.

49. As well as the gist of what they actually said: Thucydides 1.22. The bibliography exploring this formulation is endless.

50. Balcer 1989: 127 on Thucydides 1.69.5.

51. Balcer 1995: 39.

52. For an account of Herodotus' account, see Harrison 2002.

53. Kent 1953: DNb 8d 21-24.

54. Herodotus 3.76; for the Persian education in archery, riding and telling the truth, 1.136.

55. Herodotus 7.10.e2; 8.90; see further Harrison 2004.

56. Briant 2002: 2. See Lane Fox 2007 for an exhaustive (sceptical) analysis of this tag, also Wiemer 2007, focussing on Alexander's reception by the Babylonian priesthood; as Tuplin remarks, however (2008: 109), it 'serves better as an arresting image for one strand in what was inevitably a multi-strand story than as a summary of that story's overall impact'.

57. Lane Fox 2007: 268.

58. Kuhrt 1995: 675. Contrast Cawkwell 2005: 199 ('there was perhaps more strategic talent in the Persian command than Alexander's adulators allow').

59. Brosius 2003a: 170. See Briant's most recent reconstruction (2009a), from diverse sources, of the empire of Darius III, concluding (p. 168) that it was 'still an economic and administrative organisation with a logical coherence that was comparable overall with the elaborately documented structures in place during the reign of Darius I'. See also e.g. Briant 1979b, esp. 290, for a treatment of Alexander as a model for modern colonialism, Garvin 2003 for an attempt to reconstruct Darius' strategy (of staged withdrawal and counter-attack) confounded by Alexander's decision to head south after Issus, Nylander 1993, arguing that Darius' flight was to protect the association of the King with cosmic order.

60. But this is to presume that Greek historians have more stereotyped notions of the Persian empire or of Alexander than they in fact (mostly) do.

61. Brosius 2006a: 63.

62. Bosworth 1996 is a notable exception: see esp. chs 1, 6 (e.g. pp. 19-20). Ironically, Briant's own popular account of Alexander, subtitled 'The heroic ideal' (1996) is a traditional Hellenocentric account, with only a slight dig at the complacency of Greek authors' (p. 32).

63. Allen 2005a: 137.

64. Allen 2005a: 136 (my italics).

65. Brosius 2003a: 172, citing Sancisi-Weerdenburg 1993a: 185; cf. Brosius 2003a: 192 ('after crossing the Hellespont, [he] employed the same aggressive and military methods to achieve his goal and "bulldozed" his way into the Persian centre'), Allen 2005a: 133 ('The invaders' systematic vandalism of the most distinctively Persian of the four royal capitals, where the last Achaemenid kings had been buried, undermined the foundations of the monarchy's identity').

66. Brosius 2003a: 169, 173, 181; Allen 2005a: 151, in the context of the mourning ordered by Alexander for Hephaistion.

67. Shahbazi 2003: 24-5, in the context of a reconstruction of the early negative Persian reaction to Alexander.

68. Briant 2002: 120, citing DB Bab. (the Babylonian version of the Behistun inscription) 17.

69. For variant accounts, see Arrian *Anabasis* 3.18.10-12, Diodorus

Siculus 17.70-72, Plutarch *Alexander* ch. 38. See also Brosius 2003b, exposing the awkwardness in Philip's claim to avenge Persia given Macedon's part in the Persian wars ('The enmity towards Persia was created because of Persian involvement in Greek affairs. Philip's real enemy was Greece').

70. For an account of Alexander's performing 'a permanent act of ideological splits', see Harrison 2009, esp. 230-1.

71. Austin 2003: 126, the context being the diplomatic pronouncements of the Seleucid kings.

72. Cf. van der Spek's balanced reconstruction of Alexander's accommodation with Persian nobility, 2003: 341-2; cf. also Kuhrt 1990 for sensible scepticism over the allegedly jubilant reception of Alexander in Babylon, Kuhrt 1987: 49, equating Alexander's and Cyrus' accommodation with Babylon; contrast Smelik 1978/9, constructing Alexander's reception (excessively) as a liberator from 'sacrilegious Persian kings' (p. 108).

73. E.g. Brosius 2003a: 175, 187; cf. Kuhrt 2007: 421.

74. Van der Spek 2003: 341-2. Van der Spek also does not suppose 'misunderstanding and distrust' on Alexander's part towards Babylonian culture (as Smelik 1978/9: 107-8): 'who knows whether he was not really impressed by Babylonian civilisation?'

75. Bosworth 1996: 1.

76. See further below, Chapters 5 and 7. Cf. the opening observations of Dusinberre 2003: xiii; some unease concerning Persian imperialism might also be implicit in the concern of some scholars to limit the scope of imperial ideology: see below, Chapter 6.

77. See further Harrison 2008.

3. Family Fortunes

1. Herodotus 9.108-14.

2. Herodotus 1.8; for the pattern of logoi in Book 1 mirroring those of the close of the *Histories*, see e.g. Griffiths 1999.

3. For this occasion, see also Sancisi-Weerdenburg 1989b: 132-3.

4. Herodotus 9.122; cf. the more positive reading of Root 1985: 113.

5. Herodotus 7.11 (tr. Robin Waterfield).

6. Cf. Wiesehöfer 2006 for Thucydides' account as a 'fairly objective description of the history of Graeco-Persian relations' (though providing scarce information, p. 667).

7. Herodotus 7.5 (though Mardonius may also be deceitful here).

8. Cf. Sancisi-Weerdenburg 1983: 21: 'After their fatal defeats at Salamis, Plataea and Mycale the empire went downhill. The central government was no longer strong and firm. Luxury, wealth, the harem and female intrigues heavily corrupted the highest regions of the government. In Xerxes' reign women started playing all-important roles. Queens decided and kings complied with their wishes'; cf. (e.g.) Sancisi-Weerdenburg 1994a: 101, Briant 2002: 515-18, Stolper 1999: 1112; contrast the undi-

luted narrative of decadence of Brentjes 1995, pages away from Sancisi-Weerdenburg's account of Darius.

9. Though arguably too little close reading of the end of the *Histories* in their literary-historical context.

10. Kuhrt 1995: 648.

11. Keaveney 1996: 33-8; for a splendidly detailed reconstruction of the building of Xerxes' bridge (based, predominantly, on Herodotus' testimony) see Hammond 1996. The question of the Persian kings' Zoroastrianism has been a longstanding question: see the sensible summary of Sancisi-Weerdenburg 1993b: 147-50, but especially now the masterful study of Henkelman 2008, peeling back a priori assumptions of the nature of Persian religion.

12. Masson 1950, West 1987: 265-6, Rollinger 2000: 66-70. For other dimensions of the Pythius story, see S. Lewis 1998.

13. Sancisi-Weerdenburg 1980a: ch. 2, 1983: 29-30; see also Sancisi-Weerdenburg 1988a for the Persian gift of an army, 1989b for the ideology of gift-giving more generally.

14. Sancisi-Weerdenburg 1983: 29.

15. Xenophon *Agesilaus* 9.3-5; *Cyropaedia* 8.8.9-11; cf. Xenophon, *Hiero* 1.22-4, expressing some pity for the tyrant with his luxurious diet. Cf. Briant 2002: 301 for royal luxury as a statement of power.

16. Herodotus 1.133, Heracleides 689 F 2 (translated at Kuhrt 2007: 610-11). See further Sancisi-Weerdenburg 1995b, Briant 1989b, Lenfant 2009: 277-98; cf. Briant 1994a, Sancisi-Weerdenburg 1987d: 495 (on Cook 1983: 140) for the symbolism surrounding the King's water.

17. Briant 2002: 97 on Herodotus 3.35.

18. Cf. Amestris, Herodotus 7.114, with Parker 2004; cf. Sancisi-Weerdenburg 1980a: 65.

19. For an alternative approach to Cambyses' madness (and comparison with the case of the Spartan Cleomenes), see Griffiths 1989. Cambyses' brief episodes of sanity (e.g. Herodotus 3.14) – best interpreted as a function of the narrative – are given some weight by Briant 2002: 55.

20. Sancisi-Weerdenburg 1983: 20, 32.

21. In addition to the Herodotean examples cited here (e.g. 7.114), see ample examples in Ctesias' *Persica*, e.g. Ctesias 688 F 9, 13a, 14-16, 27 (cf. Plutarch *Artoxerxes* 17). In the words of Lenfant, 2004: cix, 'les exécutions ordonnés ... ne se comptent pas et elles se distinguent par la variété de leurs modalités, que Ctésias omet rarement de préciser'.

22. E.g. Herodotus 4.43, Ctesias 688 F 14, 17.

23. Herodotus 7.2-4.

24. Hellanicus of Lesbos 4 F 178a (= 687a F 7). The myths of Atossa and of Semiramis appear to have developed in a symbiotic relationship (Tuplin's phrase, 1996: 168); by attributing the innovation of correspondence justice to Atossa, Hellanicus is making her the initiator of Oriental monarchy (cf. the story of Deioces, Herodotus 1.100, discussed above, with e.g. Steiner 1994: 128-32).

25. Herodotus 8.88.
26. Wiesehöfer 1996: 83. Cf. Sancisi-Weerdenburg 1987b: 40-3, Allen 2005a: 97 ('The stories of relentless retribution enacted as the result of the interference of the Persian royal women were popular with Greek authors, who saw them as evidence of the decadence of the Achaemenid power structure. In foreigners' eyes, the profusion of women around the king was evidence of his decadence and devotion to carnal pleasures.')
27. Sancisi-Weerdenburg 1983: 20, 27.
28. Brosius 1996: 122.
29. Brosius 2006a: 41-2.
30. Wiesehöfer 1996: 85. Cf. Allen 2005a: 97 ('They owned property, travelled with entourages across the empire, and wielded seals in order to conduct business. Nevertheless, the behaviour of royal women may have been as closely watched as that of the male nobles around the king, since their role in the legitimacy of royal household was key').
31. Brosius 1996: 116; cf. pp. 118, 120.
32. In fairness, Brosius' 1996 discussion does highlight Greek ideological perspectives, though underestimating them e.g. in presenting Achaemenid women as 'used ... to fill the gap in the narratives and to add a bit of sensationalism' (p. 69).
33. Herodotus 2.100, 2.107, 4.165-7,199-205; cf. 3.119. Cf. Rollinger's survey of violence in Herodotus, 2004, concluding – somewhat mechanically – that his concern is with the association of violence with monarchy (Greek and foreign), not with distinctions between peoples.
34. Cf. Brosius 1996: 51.
35. Herodotus 1.4. Cf. the Greek tradition of Persian women commanding armies, for which see Sancisi-Weerdenburg 1988a.
36. Hdt. 3.1-3; cf. Ctesias 688 F 13a, Dinon 690 F 11, Lykeas of Naukratis 613 F 11. See further above, Chapter 2.
37. Herodotus 3.134.
38. Deinon 690 F 12.
39. D.M. Lewis 1977: 21-2. See also the balanced comments of Lenfant 2004: ccci-ii on the historicity of anecdotes concerning Parysatis, also, more broadly, Llewellyn-Jones and Robson 2010: 84-6; cf., perhaps more fancifully, Cook 1985: 225 on the psychology of absolute power ('The pinnacle of power was a lonely perch').
40. Briant 2002: 123, with good examples of violence.
41. Katouzian 2009: e.g. 8. See also Brosius 2007: 53: 'servile opportunism and flattery were undoubtedly part of everyday life at court'.
42. See Bosworth 1996: 22-3 for a well maintained balance. Ironically, it was a central scholar of the Achaemenid revival, Matt Stolper, who (with no obvious moral complexion, or irony, to his words?) paraphrased Briant's account of Darius with the words: 'Bref, Darius est un Auguste or un Stalin perse', 1999: 1116.
43. Lincoln 2007: 94-5 on Plutarch *Artoxerxes* 16.1-4.

142

44. E.g. Green 1996: 5, speaking of Persia as having 'perpetuated a fundamentally static culture, geared to the maintenance of a theocratic status quo, and hostile ... to original creativity in any form'; Persian culture', he continues, is 'almost as alien to us as that of the Aztecs' (p. 5). See further below, Chapter 6, for some popular responses.

45. The approach of Cook 1985: 288-91 in assessing 'the quality of Achaemenid administration' is arguably exemplary here (whatever the faults may be of his analysis). Cf. Briant 2008: 19, 37 (in his laborious 'open letter' to Alexander).

46. See e.g. (with clear streaks of this competitive approach) Brosius 1996: 2, 105, 106, 112.

47. Cf. Llewellyn-Jones 2002: 30.

48. Wiesehöfer 1996: 85. Cf. Brosius 2006a: 43: 'Their [Persian women's] ability to travel and their economic independence are a far cry from the Greek notion that Persian women lived in the seclusion of the palace, hidden away from the outside world'.

49. Herodotus 3.119.

50. Brosius 1996: 117. Discussion has often focussed on the similarity of the story to Sophocles *Antigone* 905-12. Contrast the reduction in the role of Atossa posited by Brosius 1996: 48-51, 108-9.

51. Brosius 1996: 69.

52. See esp. S. Lewis 2002 for an important survey of the Attic vase evidence; for the ideal of Greek women's seclusion, Llewellyn-Jones 2003, and see also the observations of Davidson 2006: 33.

53. Though cf. Brosius 1996: ch. 5 for the evidence of the Persepolis tablets for non-royal women.

54. See e.g. Sancisi-Weerdenburg 1988a: 374, Brosius 2007: 31.

55. See esp. Llewellyn-Jones 2002 (perhaps going too far towards essentialising Persian national characteristics, p. 29); for eunuchs, see Hopkins 1963, Tougher 2008 (cf. Briant 2002: 269-78). It is notable that e.g. Shahbazi 2004: 1 is matter-of-fact about the existence of the Persian harem ('The Persians made every effort to safeguard the lifestyle and honor of their women').

56. Brosius 2006a: 41 ('Herodotus' statement ... supports this assumption' [that women were in fact represented]) on Herodotus 7.69.2.

57. A lioness (on which see Root 2003). See also, however, Spycket 1980, Sancisi-Weerdenburg 1983: 22-3, warning against conclusions of the absence of women on the basis of the reliefs, Brosius 1996: 84-6, Root 2008: 207-8 (pointing out that seals, on which women are portrayed, are not private), Brosius 2010: esp. 141-2. Contrast the perspective of Sancisi-Weerdenburg 1987b: 42-3, suggesting that a focus on Greek anecdotes of Persian women as literary helps to explain their relative absence in other contexts.

58. Olmstead 1948: xi. See now Palagia 2008 for the argument, based on dating and the identification of the marble as Thasian, that the

Persephone was a diplomatic gift of the mid-fifth century rather than looted art.

59. Brosius 1996: 86.

60. Sancisi-Weerdenburg 1997: 339-40 on Persian 'haute cuisine'.

61. Sancisi-Weerdenburg 1995b: 295; cf. D.M. Lewis 1987. See now, however, Henkelman forthcoming on the absence of larger animals from the Persepolis archive. Cf. Briant 2002: 252 on Persian drunkenness (seemingly unsure whether to credit the Persians with drunkenness or to explain it in ritual terms).

62. And the Greek image of the Persian king's luxury was never, in fact, so extreme: see the observations of Lenfant 2007, Tuplin 2007: xvi, 1996: e.g. 149-50, 162, 169-70, 176.

4. Live and Let Live

1. Kuhrt and Sherwin-White 1987. Cf. Kuhrt 1983: 94, noting Xerxes' destruction more broadly.

2. Though cf. Ackroyd 1990, Gruen 2005, for a portrayal of the Persians' biblical image, which brings out less favourable aspects.

3. See below, this chapter, for refs; for the image of Xerxes' reign as a falling off, see e.g. Sancisi-Weerdenburg 1989a, Briant 2002: 550-3.

4. Sancisi-Weerdenburg 1993b: 383.

5. Herodotus 3.27-9.

6. Herodotus 3.38.

7. For texts, Kuhrt 2007: 122-4.

8. Briant 2002: 57; cf. Allen 2005a: 35.

9. See Lloyd 1982: 171.

10. Tuplin 1991: 259-61 (at p. 259).

11. See most recently Depuydt 1995.

12. See e.g. Devauchelle 1998, Cruz-Uribe 2003: 54-7; cf. Briant's confidence, 2002: 57.

13. Cruz-Uribe 2003: 43-5 (revealing, however, too black-and-white a contrast of invention and historical accuracy).

14. The so-called Demotic chronicle: Kuhrt 2007: 125. See Dillery 2005; cf. Cruz-Uribe 2003: 50 for the suggestion that his 'universal abomination ... by later authors' may have been the result of actions of Darius, e.g. the collation of Egyptian laws, 'taken ... to put himself in a better light'.

15. Translated by Kuhrt 2007: 119; this is a section elided in Brosius' sourcebook, 2000: 15.

16. Baines 1996; for a fuller context, cf. Posener 1936: 1-29.

17. Cf. Sancisi-Weerdenburg 1993b: 156-7 (citing Lloyd 1988): 'the only evidence for inconsiderate behaviour towards Egyptian customs and traditions may have been a curtailing of priestly revenues'.

18. Thiers 1995, stressing their defensive potential, Cruz-Uribe 2003: 38.

19. Briant 2002: 56-7; cf. also 2002: 484 ('the passage from Saite power to Persian dominion was not achieved without upheavals and changes').

20. Kuhrt and Sherwin-White 1987; see now Kuhrt's fierce *apologia*, 2010.

21. 'Although the traditional story of savage revenge may be exaggerated, the radical revision of the traditional argument in recent years is at least as extreme' (Waerzeggers 2003/4: 163). The chronology of revolts is also questionable: see e.g. Kuhrt 2007, following Rollinger 1993: 218-28, Tuplin 1997b: 392-403 for a survey, and most recently Waerzeggers 2003/4.

22. George 2010. My thanks to Andrew George for showing me a copy of his paper prior to publication. Cf. Kuhrt 1997: 302 ('Xerxes as the destroyer of Babylonian temples has finally been laid to rest').

23. Contrast Allen 2005a: 52, minimising the effects of Xerxes' occupation to the transfer of tracts of land (though 'Herodotus delighted in passing on stories about the greedy designs on Babylon held by both Xerxes and his father Darius').

24. Waerzeggers 2003/4; see also now Baker 2008 on evidence of disruption in the Merkes residential district of Babylon, Kuhrt 2010 for reconciliation with Kuhrt and Sherwin-White 1987.

25. Briant 2002: 56-7.

26. Cf. Xerxes' propitiation of Athenian gods on the Acropolis, after burning its temples: Herodotus 8.53-4.

27. Cf. Kuhrt 2007: 130n.3.

28. Briant 2002: 59-61: 'Whatever it was, the royal decision need not be considered a contradiction of the general policy applied to the Egyptians' (p. 61).

29. I should insist that I am not arguing here for a return to the model of 'nationalistic' resistance and isolated acts of collaboration in Egypt that is satirised by Briant 2001, 1988: 139. Briant's analysis, 1988, of the complex causes of Egyptian revolts seems eminently balanced.

30. Briant 2002: 59.

31. Austin 2003: 126. See further, in the same volume, the emphasis of Ma 2003: 182-3 on the dynamic negotiation between king and local population (in the context of Hellenistic kingdoms, but with explicit parallels being drawn to the Achaemenid past).

32. See e.g. Devauchelle 1995, Briant 1988: 170-1 emphasising e.g. class distinction, Ray 1987 for an elegiac account of the last century of Egyptian independence in the fourth century.

33. Holm-Rasmussen 1988. And the Persian King may only passively have conformed to the role: as emphasised by Lloyd 2007: 104, or Tuplin 2007: xix, the Egyptians needed a pharaoh, 'so assimilation of Darius (or any other Achaemenid) into an Egyptian discourse is not a judgement on that king's actual or perceived attitude to Egypt' (in the words of Tuplin).

34. XPh, translated by Kuhrt (2007: 305).

35. And see, more recently, Brentjes 1995: 1020 (pages away from

145

contrary views of Sancisi-Weerdenburg 1995a: 1049), Abdi 2010: e.g. 283 (pp. 279-84 for a history of past interpretations of the text).

36. E.g. Sancisi-Weerdenburg 1980a: 31, 1993b: 158, Henkelman 2008: 10; the time-frame for the commotion referred to is difficult to fix as the Old Persian aorist and imperfect were used indiscriminately (Sancisi-Weerdenburg 1999: 97).

37. Cf. Allen 2005a: 53: 'The worship of "daivas" is used here to describe rebellion, in a way similar to Darius' use of the moral absolute of the "lie" to explain the actions of those who did not accept his rule'; cf. Briant 2002: 12-16 on Behistun.

38. Brosius 2006a: 68: 'Yet in any case, it is important to note that the cult of Ahuramazda will not be imposed on the people, but that Xerxes will worship Ahuramazda there – a significant distinction'. For an alternative reading, placing the inscription in the context of Zoroastrian eschatology, see Kellens 1969.

39. Herodotus 6.19; for Persian threats, 6.9, for which see below, Chapter 6.

40. Allen 2005a: 55.

41. Sancisi-Weerdenburg 1993b: 381.

42. Henkelman 2008: 342.

43. E.g. Herodotus 5.105, 7.8. The religious discourse of Persian imperialism is a recurrent theme of Lincoln 2007, e.g. 76; see more fully Ahn 1992.

44. Brosius 2006a: 65; cf. Allen 2005a: 131 ('Persian religious tolerance was a result of an inclusive imperial ideology, but it was a tactic of domination and could still work well for some, harshly for others'). From a different perspective, cf. Katouzian 2009: 31 on the Cyrus Cylinder as '[proclaiming] the freedom of his subject peoples in matters of religion and culture'.

45. Sancisi-Weerdenburg 1982: 274; a briefer statement to the same effect was made by Sancisi-Weerdenburg in the advertisement of the first colloquium, 1980b: 230-1. See also Briant 1979a: 1409-10, Wiesehöfer 1996: 55, and (for the most sophisticated expression) Sancisi-Weerdenburg 2001a: 334-7. Henkelman 2008: 35-51 offers a critique of the idea of tolerance of Elamite gods on the basis that there is no evidence that they are seen as a distinct group (from Iranian divinities).

46. Sancisi-Weerdenburg 1982: 279; cf. Lane Fox 2006: 166, in the context of upholding the authenticity of the Gadatas letter (see n. 47 below): 'To polytheists, local gods were real gods and if they spoke "the truth" to the King and favoured him, he would favour them too.' Instead of referring to a policy of tolerance, Kuhrt more cautiously writes of the Kings' [anxiety] 'to maintain the privileges of cultic communities', 1983: 94.

47. Meiggs and Lewis 1988: no. 12. The letter's authenticity has been challenged, most recently by Briant 2003b; see, however, two compelling responses, Lane Fox 2006, Tuplin 2009.

48. For a graphic illustration, the substitution of Bel for Ahuramazda in the Behistun text, see Henkelman 2008: 336.

49. Brosius 2006a: 50.

50. Brosius 2006a: 50 (cf. Briant's sensible observations on multilingualism, 2002: 77); I am more sceptical of Brosius' claim that it was a way of 'integrating the different peoples by not appearing as an oppressing power'. Cf. Brosius 2006a: 1-2: 'To a large extent this [the empire's lasting] was due to the Persian kings' acceptance of the political, cultural and religious diversity of the different peoples of the lands of the empire. No attempt was made to impose Persian language and religion on other people. Instead , the kings emphasised a policy which was, to use a modern phrase, all-inclusive. This does not mean to say that there were no repercussions in case of rebellious activities, but in principle the political and religious tolerance of the Achaemenid kings towards their subject peoples was adhered to, and was, by all accounts, overwhelmingly successful.'

51. Root 1991: 6.

52. Nylander 1979: 346.

53. Kuhrt 2001: 168.

54. See e.g. Briant 1988: 137, Brosius 2007: 35-9; cf. Walser 1984:20-6, Briant 2002: 348-9, for the subordinate position of Greeks in Persepolis. For the role of the satrap (and Greek knowledge of satrapies), see now the study of Klinkott 2005.

55. Tuplin 1987: 109; cf. Aperghis 2000, painting a very negative picture of the lot of war captives.

56. Allen 2005a: 68.

57. Nylander 1979: 356. If Nylander is describing a Persian aspiration, or Persian ideology, it is at least unclear: he introduces this quotation with the words 'In the Achaemenid "ideology of commonwealth", so eloquently propagandized in the reliefs, it would be very useful and efficient to create the palace in the capital as a kind of "palais des nations" ...'. Cf. Root 1990: 134: 'Persepolis was an environment calculated by its imperial patron to induce responses among peoples of the empire from near and far'; Root 2007: 210-11, asking whether 'the planners' aimed 'to provoke positive, empire-affirming responses among the Yauna ... or ... to insult and psychologically destabilize them'; their aim, she concludes, was to incorporate, but they may have failed through their effeminising representations of the Greeks.

58. Nylander 1979: 354-5. As Tuplin points out (forthcoming), the 'Apadana representatives of the entire empire are balanced in space and importance by representatives just of the court entourage. So, there is great inequality.'

59. Bedford 2007: 322: 'Respect for the cults of subjugated territories, and the fostering of an imperial ideology that encouraged a view of mutual benefit (reciprocity) all enhanced the opportunity for economic perform-

ance'; cf., however, p. 325 on the lack of evidence that political integration led to trade.

60. See e.g. Briant 1989a; cf. the formula of Sancisi-Weerdenburg 2001a: 340 ('Persians on Greeks are really Greeks on Persians and therefore Greeks on Greeks').

61. Root 1979: 147-61; cf. Root 1980: 12 ('an Achaemenid vision of ideal imperial order in which unfettered men of the empire join in cooperative praise of the King of Kings'). Root is in other contexts, however (e.g. 1979: 2), very clear on the distinction between royal ideology and the reality of 'brutal wars'.

62. DNa 3-4. Cf. Briant 2002: 178 ('the accent is placed more on political subjugation and imposition of tribute than on collaboration').

63. Brosius 2006a: 35; see further Tuplin's contrast between Assyrian and Persian imperialism, forthcoming (drawing on Parpola 2003), and for violent themes amongst seal images. Contrast Kuhrt's refutation of the 'assumption that Persian imperial control was somehow more tolerable than the Assyrian yoke', 1983: 940-5: it is an assumption 'based, on the one hand, on the limited experience of one influential group of a very small community which happened to benefit by Persian policy and, on the other, on a piece of blatant propaganda successfully modelled on similar texts devised to extol a representative and practitioner of the earlier and much condemned Assyrian imperialism'.

64. Brosius 2006a: 60; cf. p. 74. See also Stronach 1997a: 43-4 on the 'pacific tenor of Achaemenid palace art'.

65. Cf. Kuhrt 2001: 168: 'Although there were no carved depictions of scenes of conquest at Persepolis ... of course, the Persian kings repeatedly stress that their empire has been created by war'; contrast Nylander 1979: 346 ('conflict and conquest are hinted at only in vague and general terms'). For the concept of the *pax persica*, see now Brosius 2005.

66. Cf. Sancisi-Weerdenburg 1999.

67. Root 1990: 122. Cf. Jamzadeh 1995: 12 for an interpretation of why it is only on the platform of Darius' tomb at Naqsh-i-Rustam that the Persian hero kills the monster.

68. Root 1990: 121-2; cf. Root 1985: 111 (on 'imminent convergence', in the context of a comparison between the Apadana reliefs and the Parthenon frieze).

69. Briant 2002: 122 on Herodotus 3.126; cf. Dusinberre 2003: 197, interpreting the episode (equally literally) as evidence of the power of Darius' 'personal charisma'.

70. See e.g. Briant 2002: 152, emphasising a groundswell of desire for isonomia and minimising anti-Persian feeling (with which it was associated); cf. Graf 1985, minimising anti-tyrannical feeling at this time, and supposing the Greeks 'compliant, perhaps even invertebrate' (p. 99). Contrast Austin 1990: 289: 'There can be little doubt that one of the major grievances behind the revolt was a resentment widely felt, at least in Ionia proper and

in Lesbos, for which we have specific evidence, against the individual Greeks who ruled as tyrants there, and whose rule was felt to be dependent on Persian support.'

71. Briant 2002: 159.

72. See below, Chapter 6.

73. Cf. Austin 2003: 126 on the 'balance of pressures at any given time'.

74. Gruen 2005: 102. Cf., in more condensed style, Tuplin forthcoming: 'Yahweh gets the credit for Achaemenid power while Jewish figures manipulate Persian rulers and make them look silly.'

75. Lloyd 2007: 106; the fact of the text being set up (according to Egyptian precedent) is some concession to the Egyptian context. For the Suez canal more broadly, see Tuplin 1991, stressing its symbolic rather than economic role. See also Tuplin forthcoming on the Persian psychological reaction of 'triumphalist *apartheid*'.

76. DSz; cf. DSab. For the requirement placed on satraps to extend Persian power, see e.g. Briant 2002: 65, again citing Oroetes (Herodotus 3.120).

5. *Terra Incognita*

1. As acknowledged by Briant 1979a. See also Briant 2005 for the characterisation of Iranian historiography at the time of Ernst Herzfeld's death (in 1948) as 'blossoming', or his citation with approval of Olmstead 1948: 524 (Briant 2005: 277): 'Now, at last, through the united effort of archaeologist, philologist, and historian, Achaemenid Persia has risen from the dead.'

2. Cf. Raimond 2007: 143, describing Hallock 1969 as 'in retrospect a major landmark'.

3. As suggested to me by Christopher Tuplin. This is certainly borne out by the Syndics of Cambridge University Press allowing the publication of Hallock 1971 in advance of volume 2 of the *Cambridge History of Iran* (on the Achaemenid period), eventually published in 1985: this special publication was intended 'as a token of what is to come, to mark an anniversary unique in the history the course of which the Board [of editors] were set up to survey' (Ilya Gershevitz's preface to Hallock 1971: 1). Cf. Cook 1983: iii, crediting the doubling of scholarship in the 1970s to the anniversary and to the publication of the archives.

4. Cf. Allen's formulation, 2005a: 6, that 'specialised study' has developed 'more recently'. See above, Preface, for further acknowledgements of work previous to 1980.

5. Sancisi-Weerdenburg 1991: 2 ('Curzon did pioneering work in collecting a large number of travellers' descriptions and his lists are still a good starting point'); cf. the more positive treatment of Curzon by Stronach, e.g. 1978: 24-5, or Boardman 2000: 9. Gunter and Hauser, 2005: 5, characterise

Henry Rawlinson's work at Behistun as marking the beginning of 'academic studies of the field'; cf. Mousavi 2003: 220 on Curzon as 'mark[ing] the end of the prescientific era of archaeology at Persepolis'.

6. Kuhrt and Sancisi-Weerdenburg 1987: ix-x. Cf. Briant 2005: 267-8: 'The internal development of the Achaemenid Empire was considered almost unanimously as a long decay after the defeats in the Persian Wars.'

7. Curzon 1892: i.12.

8. Brosius 1990; see also Bowden 1998: 101-5, contrasting Gillies and Mitford.

9. Curzon 1892; for a narrative of Curzon's travels, see Bosworth 1993.

10. See Simpson 2003: 192, in context of an excellent sketch of the variety of professional contexts of travellers; more fully, Wright 2001.

11. Cf. the similar emphasis of Sancisi-Weerdenburg 1991(a survey of travellers focussing on the purported ceremonial function of Persepolis). Contrast the caricature of nineteenth-century scholarship as focussing on the negative of Razmjou 2008 (or restated in interview, *Financial Times Magazine*, 3-4 Sept. 2005, p. 34).

12. G. Rawlinson 1885: 502.

13. Olmstead 1948: 266-7. Root, 1979: 91, surprisingly describes decisions on royal successions as 'being made through harem intrigues and power struggles'.

14. See e.g. Sancisi-Weerdenburg's scathing review of Cook 1983: 1987d, esp. 491-2. For a defence against the 'constant "Cook-bashing"' of the early volumes of the Achaemenid History Workshop, see Hornblower 1990. There is no inevitability to Cook's narrative of the later years of the empire (1983: ch. 18), no excessive decadence to his description of the court (ch. 13); though he takes some questionable stories at face value, it is arguable that his underlying approach to the Greek sources (that Herodotus' *Histories* contain 'a firm substratum of genuine historical knowledge', 1985: 205) is not so different from that of e.g. Briant's 'noyau informatif'.

15. E.g. Sancisi-Weerdenburg 1987c: 128-31; cf. Briant's marked appreciation of Olmstead, 2005: 277. See, however, Sancisi-Weerdenburg 1983 for a broader account of Persian decadence, including esp. National Socialist representations, Wiesehöfer 1996: 86-7, Briant 2005: 267-8 (focussing also on Nöldeke, Darmesteter, and Justi), 2009b for accounts of the decadence of Darius III's empire.

16. Grundy 1901: 1-2; cf. G. Rawlinson 1885: 298 ('the causes of military success and political advance lie deeper than statistics can reach ... they have their roots in the moral nature of man, in the grandeur of his ideas and the energy of his character ...').

17. Jackson 1906: 26 ('Signs of weakness had already shown themselves ... in the unsuccessful attempt of Darius to invade Greece, but these marks of decadence became more and more manifest in the reigns of Xerxes and Artaxerxes, until the tottering throne of the Achaemenidae fell when Darius

III (Codomannus) was conquered by Alexander the Great and afterward perished ...').

18. Jackson 1906: 322. For Jackson's pioneering role in US Iranian studies, see Malandra 2008.

19. P.M. Sykes 1922: 18-19.

20. P.M. Sykes 1922: 20ff. ('The overthrow of the Persian empire by Alexander ranks high among the greatest achievements of man'); cf. Kuhrt 1995: 675 ('It was a remarkable achievement, and the difficulties Alexander encountered in twelve years of continuous fighting bear witness to the remarkable solidity of the Achaemenid realm').

21. Cf. Sancisi-Weerdenburg 1987a: xi: 'in treatises on the Persian Empire it is commonplace to assert that after Xerxes' death in 465 the whole Empire gradually underwent a process of decay that made it a ready prey for the Macedonian conquests'; cf. Sancisi-Weerdenburg 1989a.

22. Kinneir 1813: 76; cf. p. 51 ('In sculpture and painting, the Persians have at no time attained any degree of perfection. Even the figures at Persepolis, and other parts of the country, are deficient in taste and proportion; with the exception of some of those in the plain of Kermanshah, which I believe to have been executed by Grecian or Roman artists').

23. G. Rawlinson 1885: 317; cf. p. 380.

24. de Windt 1891: 172: 'The Pyramids, Pompeii, the ancient buildings of Rome and Greece, are picturesque; Persepolis is not.'

25. Bradley-Birt 1909: 180. Cf., in an earlier period, the eulogy of Sir William Ouseley, 1819-23: ii.288-9.

26. Berenson 1954: 186 (cited by Nylander 1970: 148).

27. See esp. Root 1979, 1991, Nylander 1970.

28. Curzon 1892: i. 194; see also e.g. the Orientalist Denison Ross, e.g. 1931: 103 ('Most of the elements which went to make up these palaces were borrowed from Greek, Babylonian, and Egyptian models, but each element received a touch of originality at the hands of the Persians').

29. Millspaugh 1925: 4-5; cf. Arnold 1877: 331-2.

30. Morton 1940: 175.

31. Collins 1896: 78-9 (for the Democedes comparison, pp. 270-1).

32. Curzon 1892: ii.161; cf. Root 1985.

33. Fergusson, quoted approvingly by Arnold 1877: 331-2.

34. Benjamin 1887: 336-7: 'I think that those who have given attention to the music of ancient Greece might gain a clearer perception of that subject by investigating the native music of Persia. Indeed it would not be surprising if it should be found that the Dorians borrowed from the Greek colonies of Asia Minor, who in turn borrowed their music from the Persians. Both were of Aryan stock. We know that neither the Persian nor the Greek of antiquity disdained to borrow customs and ideas from each other. Why then should the Greek not have borrowed music from the Persians?'

35. G. Rawlinson 1885: 412.

36. Cf. Root 1979: 7, acknowledging Herzfeld's role in 'leading the

Orientalists' in maintaining the Near Eastern nature of Persian art; it may also be, of course, that Richter's judgment became 'canonized' (as Root 1980: 9) – though this is difficult to gauge without a more systematic treatment of the theme in twentieth-century scholarship. Contrast also the narrative of modern views on Persian art of Briant 2005: 270-2, focussing on Perrot and Chipiez, and emphasising continuity in negative views (citing Frankfort 1946 and Richter 1946) 'despite the progress made during Herzfeld's time'.

37. Pope 1938: 15. Cf. Herzfeld 1941, seeing Persia (p. 221) as on the 'path of civilization: Asia Minor, Urartu, Media, Persis', for whom (against a background of central control of the Persepolitan artistic programme) 'the question as to whether some foreign artists took part in its creation becomes entirely insignificant' (p. 274); cf. 1941: 233 ('this Egyptian ornament does not make Persian art Egyptian any more than the fluting of the columns makes it Greek'), Herzfeld 1935: 44. For Herzfeld's idea of the death of 'Ancient East', however, see 1941: 274.

38. Casson 1938: 346, 350, Wachtsmuth 1938: 320.

39. Casson 1938: 365, Unvala 1938: 337.

40. Casson 1938: 359; cf. p. 363 expressing doubts that seals were made by Greeks for Persians.

41. Cooke 1938: 395, in the context of a rapturous appreciation of their 'delicacy, almost miraculously exquisite' (p. 394). Cf. Margaret Cool Root's observation on 'Graeco-Persian' in the preface to Kaptan 2002: 'Its polarising rubrics ... no longer seem sustainable' (p. xiv), or the excellent piece of Gates 2003, advocating a focus on 'situational' rather than ethnic identity in artistic production.

42. Malcolm 1815: 621; cf. e.g. Benjamin 1887: 169, de Lorey and Sladen 1907: vii, Anderson 1880: vii, or the illustrations labelled 'The past in the present' in Olmstead 1948 (chosen by Olmstead's daughter).

43. This catalogue of timeless vices and virtues is not, of course, absolutely consistent: appreciation of Persian wit, for example, is sometimes clearly more than merely formulaic: e.g. in the case of Browne 1926 or the letters of Edward Burgess 1942; rarely also Persian characteristics are seen as mutable, esp. by later writers such as Millspaugh 1925: 98, Meritt-Hawkes 1935: 87-8. But, for the most part, such stereotypes are replicated seamlessly, writers find confirmation of 'ideas that predate travel' (see Gikandi 1996: ch. 2), and an imaginary Persia becomes authoritative. So e.g. Hajji Baba of Ispahan (the fictional creation of J.J. Morier, 1824) is noted by many writers to be 'truer than much that purports to be fact' (e.g. G. Fowler 1841: i.48, Mounsey 1872: iv, Williams 1907: 3, Millspaugh 1925: 23), with Sykes engineering a translation into Persian for use by the Indian government to teach Indians proper Persian, P.M. Sykes 1902: 8n.2.

44. E.g. G. Rawlinson 1885: 316, Browne 1926: 309, Ross 1931: 27.

45. Malcolm 1815: 637-8.

46. E.g. Kinneir 1813: 22-3, G. Rawlinson 1885: 319 ('the love of finesse and intrigue [which] is congenital to Orientals'), Anderson 1880: 66-7, 233.

47. E.g. P.M. Sykes 1915: 181-7, Anderson 1880: 274, Bassett 1886: 50.

48. E.g. G. Rawlinson 1885: 319 (finding 'Aeschylus' tragedy of the "Persae" ... in this respect, true to nature'), Bell 1928: 55 ('To the Englishman, tears are a serious matter').

49. Malcolm 1815: 637-8.

50. A recent history of Iran by an Iranian, for example, regularly recites timeless Iranian characteristics: Katouzian 2009 (e.g. p. 18: 'Iranians as a people are intelligent, inventive and artistic. They are versatile and adaptable to different situations. They love fun, gaiety, and outdoor activity. They almost make an art of eating', and so on).

51. Marchand 2009: 24.

52. Nonetheless, there are a number of ill-defined strategies for maintaining the idea of continuity. One is to hold to the racial distinction: modern-day Zoroastrians, Parsees or Guebers are the pure Iranians and in some sources seen as more honest, hard-working, essentially Protestant than their Muslim neighbours (e.g. Price 1832: 34, Mounsey 1872: 152-3, E.C. Sykes 1898: 143, P.M. Sykes 1902: 198; cf. Bassett 1886: 316). Alternatively other Aryans may have taken on the mantle of empire? Or there may be some hope of renaissance, whether it be broadly political (in the light e.g. of the constitutional movement and Reza Shah's coup: Rice 1916: 41, 185-6, Williams 1907: 255-7, E.C. Sykes 1910: 38, 340, Millspaugh 1925: 4-5, Merritt-Hawkes 1935: 87-8, Morton 1940: 173, 355) or religious (Islam is frequently seen as no more than a vehicle for other feelings – a 'loose garment that may be fitted to any occasion without pinching', Benjamin 1887: 96; cf. Arnold 1877: 484, 491 – despite the lack of penetration of Christian missionaries).

53. G. Rawlinson 1885: 316, 444.

54. For this question of the Zoroastrian status of Achaemenid Persia, once dominant (e.g. Duchesne-Guillemin 1972), see the summary of Sancisi-Weerdenburg 1993b: 147-50; for Persian religion, now above all, Henkelman 2008.

55. G. Rawlinson 1885: 425; cf. Rice 1916: 11. For an account of the relationship of Persia and Judaism in German scholarship, see Marchand 2009: 279-84.

56. Ross 1931: 31.

57. P.M. Sykes 1915: 187; P.M. Sykes 1902: 198 pursues a similar racial distinction (adding the twist that the Bombay Parsees exemplify 'the physical deterioration which India so surely produces'); cf. Ross 1931: 35, Benjamin 1887: 88.

58. G. Rawlinson 1885: 315.

59. Durand 1902: 142.

60. Bradley-Birt 1909: 183.

61. Bradley-Birt 1909: 200-1; cf. P.M. Sykes 1902: 325.

62. Jackson 1906: 146, 200-1, 278; cf. Ross 1931: 6, Amory 1929: 49 (on Pasargadae: 'one solitary column bathing in a sunbeam and proclaiming more loudly than words departed and historic grandeur').

63. Root 1979: 311.

64. Malcolm 1827: ii.236; cf. Williams 1907: 188, 215. Contrast the emotional link posited between Persians and Persepolis by Morton 1940: 173 ('This is a close, deep feeling, due to their racial identification with all that Persepolis signifies, and their belief that in their time, or in that of their children, Iran will again be great').

65. Baker 1876: 127.

66. Bradley-Birt 1909: 181; Denison Ross makes a contrast with the Greeks, 1931: 34.

67. Moore 1915: 352 (see also the captions to Moore's illustrations of Cyrus' tomb and the palace of Xerxes: respectively, 'Goats and children guard the tomb that Alexander entered with reverence', '"the wild ass stamps over his head"' – a quotation from Fitzgerald's Omar Khayyam – or the illustration of Cyrus' tomb at Williams 1907: 230-1); cf. Bradley-Birt 1909: 223, 228, Carroll 1960: 45-6 (Behistun), 62 (Persepolis).

68. Williams 1907: 231.

69. Browne 1926: 277; see now Razmjou 2005 for Sasanian graffiti at Persepolis, Allen 2007 for Iranian reception of Persepolis, Mousavi 2003 for the role of Iranians in its excavation.

70. And, in the more optimistic view of some twentieth-century writers (see above, n. 52), appreciation of their heritage is envisaged as a path to 'independent prosperity': see Williams 1907: 231, Merritt-Hawkes 1935: 87-8 ('The Persians come to Persepolis to gain courage to forge ahead with the modernization of their country').

71. G. Fowler 1841: ii.44-5.

72. Curzon 1892: i.10.

73. Baker 1876: 336.

74. Bradley-Birt 1909: 323-4.

75. Benjamin 1887: 489.

76. G. Rawlinson 1885: 433; cf. p. 447.

77. G. Rawlinson 1885: 467; conversely, Sir John Malcolm finds the root of all Persia's problems in her lack of a proper civil administration, 1815: 637-8.

78. G. Rawlinson 1885: 474; Bradley-Birt is unusually most attracted to the Sassanian kings, 1909: 90; cf. p. 78.

79. E.g. Sackville-West 1926: 86, 99-100 ('we are at the mercy of snow and flood, and ... of limp Oriental methods'); contrast Benjamin 1887: 469 ('I heartily advise those who wish to enjoy horse-back travelling and camping-out to try Persia').

80. P.M. Sykes 1915: 180. American travellers, by contrast, focus on the Persian royal road as a splendid mod con: e.g. Millspaugh 1925: 6 (a 'transportation wonder of the ancient world'), Amory 1929: 52.

81. Morier 1816: 135.
82. Curzon 1892: ii.153-4; two other fine comparisons (not mentioned by Curzon) are between Persepolis and the Houses of Parliament (Anderson 1880: 149-51) and between Cyrus' tomb and a dog kennel (Amory 1929: 50).
83. G. Rawlinson 1885: 419.
84. Jackson 1906: 3; cf. P.M. Sykes 1902: 4-5.
85. P.M. Sykes 1915: xi-xii.
86. Cf. P.M. Sykes 1922, emphasising the influence of Zoroastrianism 'on Judaism, and indirectly on Christianity' (p. 16). His emphasis (p. 4) on 'how deeply Persia has influenced Europe' is undermined by the examples given: 'We owe to her the peach ... the orange, the lime, the pistachio nut, and possibly the vine. Of flowers, the jasmine, lilac, and narcissus not only come from Persia but have retained their Persian names, as have most of the fruits enumerated above.'
87. P.M. Sykes 1915: 180.
88. Olmstead 1948. See also Olmstead 1938: 305: 'While Persia was undoubtedly the controlling factor of contemporary Greece, the Greeks on the western frontier were for long of small interest to Persian great kings.'
89. Memorably by Eastwick 1864: 36-7. For Graves' 'Persian version', see above, Chapter 2.
90. 1846: 48: 'Xerxes, the successor of Darius, inherited to a certain extent his father's passion for Petroglyphy; but the ambition of perpetuating the victories of the Persian arms, which was the useful and ennobling object of the one, appears to have yielded, in the other, to a mere gratification of personal vanity ... .'
91. H. Rawlinson 1846: 187-8.
92. Eastwick 1864: 26-7; likely to be the same individual as the Lieutenant Eastwick who assisted Rawlinson: H. Rawlinson 1846: 175n.1.
93. Denison Ross, in the 1926 edition of Browne's *A Year Amongst the Persians*, vii: 'outside his year in Persia his life was singularly devoid of adventure, and in the events of that year his biographer can add nothing to what he has himself related so vividly'; see further Bosworth 1995.
94. Browne 1926: 5-8.
95. G. Rawlinson 1898: 22-4.
96. Quoted in Lambton 1995: 99.
97. Malcolm 1815: x; see also e.g. Ouseley 1819-23, Price 1832, and for further examples of nineteenth-century appropriation of Persian legendary past, Briant 2005: 274-5.
98. Malcolm 1815: i.16.
99. Cf. Sancisi-Weerdenburg 1987c: 128-31, criticising G. Rawlinson.
100. So, in the context of the tradition that the young Zal was nurtured by a griffin, he comments (in a footnote) that 'It is possibly to this fable that Grecian historians allude when they relate that Achaemenes was nurtured by an eagle': Malcolm 1815: i.25. In his later *Sketches of Persia*, Malcolm

seems almost to be suppressing his classical education as a sport, disarmingly suspending discussion e.g. of whether Persepolis was a palace or a temple ('I am much too wise to venture on speculations which have bewildered so many learned men') merely to report in Herodotean fashion a lengthy conversation, irrelevant to that narrow question, on the hero Rustam: Malcolm 1827: i.212.

101. Quoted by Lambton 1995: 101.

102. See e.g. Llewellyn-Jones and Robson 2010: 84.

103. The classic formulation of which is John Buchan's Sandy Arbuthnot, esp. in *Greenmantle* (1916). Actual attempts at impersonation in the Persian context include Henry Rawlinson's at Kum (G. Rawlinson 1898: 39), P.M. Sykes' disguise as a Cossack (Wynn 2003: 11-13), and Col. Charles Stewart (Stewart 1911). See, however, Fromkin 1991 for a sceptical approach, citing T.E. Lawrence ('I've never heard an Englishman speak Arabic well enough to be taken for a native of any part of the Arabic-speaking world, for five minutes'); it is notable that e.g. Stewart chose to disguise himself as an Armenian (1911: x-xi). Cf. George Rawlinson's claim that neither Herodotus nor Xenophon ('neither the lively Halicarnassian, nor the pleasant but somehow shallow Athenian') 'had the gift of penetrating very deeply into the inner mind of a foreign people', 1885: 421).

104. Curzon 1892: i.3-4.

105. G. Rawlinson 1885: 433, 447; cf. Benjamin's judgement on modern Persians, 1887: 489, that 'with Orientals everything depends upon their leaders'.

106. E.g. H. Rawlinson 1846: 190 on Darius: 'in his huge and unwieldy empire, formed of a multitude of nations, who in religion, in language, in manners, and in feelings acknowledged no one solitary bond of union, Darius was not destined to enjoy any long period of repose'. For a similar imperialist anxiety, projected onto the Roman empire, see Harrison 2008: 5-6 on Cromer and Bryce.

107. Cf. the observations of Marchand 2009: xx; see also p. 462 on Herzfeld.

108. This struggle is well brought out by Eduard Meyer, cited by Marchand 2009: 201-2: 'Small wonder that one resisted accepting [this new information]: how much we had erred, how much of the Greek information in particular – apart from the fragments of Berossus – turned out to be historically worthless data, one could not until then have imagined. This explains why so many scholars lacked the intellectual elasticity to test and incorporate the new [evidence] without preconceptions ....'

109. Kuhrt 1991: 205.

6. Concluding Hostilities

1. *Evening Standard, Life*, 7 Sept. 2005, p. 9.
2. *Guardian, G2*, 12 Oct. 2005, pp. 22-3.

3. E.g. *Sunday Times* magazine, 14 Aug. 2005, pp. 20-6, *Mail on Sunday* 11 Sept. 2005, p. 64.

4. *Spectator*, 24 Sept. 2005, pp. 73-4.

5. *Guardian*, 8 Sept. 2005, p. 10.

6. *Apollo*, Nov. 2005, pp. 80-1.

7. *Sunday Telegraph*, 18 Sept. 2005, p. 6.

8. The blogger, 'Heraclitean fire'.

9. *Spectator*, 8 Oct. 2005, p. 24.

10. 1987a: xii; cf. also Sancisi-Weerdenburg 1990a: 258 for a justification of examining reception history as a way of exploring received ideas.

11. Hornblower 1990: 94.

12. Cf. Briant 2001 on the marginalised state of Achaemenid studies: 'It must be admitted that Achaemenid research still suffers from persistent marginalization in the academic world ... presenting a doctoral dissertation on Achaemenid history is not a viable way of obtaining a university post.' Though the statistical sample is arguably too small, this is not obviously borne out by the pattern in the United Kingdom.

13. Hornblower 1990: 94.

14. See e.g. Allen 2005a: 98: 'These colourful court tales contributed to an overwhelming Orientalist tradition about the Persian monarchy. But they may also give us an idea of the social ideals governing the lives of those around the king.' Cf. Briant's swift summarising of the *topos* of Persian decadence since Xerxes, 2003a: 567.

15. See e.g. Katouzian 2009: 29, 34-6, 176.

16. Cf. Hornblower 1990: 93-4, summarising Weiskopf 1989, suggesting that the Satraps' revolt of the 360s may have been 'nothing worse than a manifestation of instability at a level which the Persians could cope with'.

17. As Christopher Tuplin points out to me, the relentless focus on the King's Peace and its renewals in Oxford 'Greats' Ancient History never suggested the feebleness of the Persian threat in the fourth century; see also Cawkwell 2005: v, 'modestly claim[ing] to have shared' the (un-Hellenocentric) view of the Achaemenid History Workshop. Conversely, a positive view of Persian stability can be found in an unlikely source such as Strauss and Ober 1990: 21.

18. Cf. again Hornblower 1990: 94: 'This [the Persian failure to reconquer Egypt], it seems to me, remains a powerful indictment.' See also Petit 1993, reintroducing a diachronic element into the narrative of Persian history (refuted disproportionately by Briant 1994b), or the realistic acknowledgement of the deep-seated problems of the reign of Darius II of Sancisi-Weerdenburg 1996: 51.

19. Cawkwell 2005: 199-213.

20. The implication perhaps of D.M. Lewis 1977: 25-6 ('there will be revelations to come about the influence of its heavy machinery'), citing e.g. *Ezra* V17-VI2; cf. D.M. Lewis 1990: 5, Hallock 1971: 31, Briant 2002: 425 ('elaborate as the system was, it gave rise to disputes'), Aperghis 1997 for

the Persians' 'optimum inventory control', Kuhrt 2007: 786-7 for evidence of 'administrative failings'. An essential starting point for discussion now is Henkelman 2008: 136-62 on the 'process of administration' of the Persepolis fortification archive.

21. Austin 2003: 128: see also Tuplin 2008: esp. 109, 123 for a counterweight to the view of continuity.

22. Root 1991: 5.

23. Haubold 2007: 52: Cf. Sancisi-Weerdenburg 2001a: 334 (for subtlety of the Persian use of foreign myth), Root 1990: 130 on the Cyrus Cylinder. Cf. Abdi 2010: 283 on Darius' pragmatic conversion to tolerance: 'people were allowed to carry on with their beliefs and practices as long as they paid their tribute on time and demonstrated their obedience to the imperial authority'.

24. See above, Chapter 2. For latest archaeological research answering the question of 'whether the Achaemenid empire existed', see Briant and Boucharlat 2005.

25. Sancisi-Weerdenburg 1990b: 263. Cf. Boardman 2000: 224 ('Nor does the growing catalogue of Persian effects, archaeological and historical, prove much when there is so very much else which demonstrates how little the way of life and even the visual experience of the Persian subject peoples had changed, or how much they were still being affected by non-Persian manners, including Greek in most western areas').

26. Root 1991: 3.

27. Root 1991: 5; cf. Briant 1988: 172-3.

28. See esp. Root 1991, Dusinberre 2003; for Achaemenid-inspired eclecticism, Dusinberre 2003: 76, for Lydian ethnicity as happily simultaneous to an 'acceptance of unifying hegemony', p. 143.

29. Sancisi-Weerdenburg 1990b: 264-7, Allen 2005b on the 'customizing response to Achaemenid iconography' (p. 59): 'The idea and image of the royal audience offered a universal space in a multi-ethnic empire for an imaginative investment in imperial rule'; for the dissemination of the audience-scene also Brosius 2010.

30. See here Root's 1997 discussion of the evidence of seals from the Persepolis archive, to show 'the complex chains of intercultural visual stimuli charging the energy field of the Persian empire' (p. 240).

31. Cf. the important discussion of the empire's impact of Tuplin forthcoming: 'it still needs stressing that the imprint is globally modest and locally variable and that we have to figure out its relative impact within particular cultural environments'.

32. Sancisi-Weerdenburg 2001a: 334: 'Persian culture was ill-suited to the needs of a large multi-ethnic empire'. Cf. Brosius 2006a: 39, rather optimistically, on the role of the Old Persian script in uniting the Persian noble class (contrast Tuplin forthcoming: 'If invention of a means of writing OP had ever been thought to have potential beyond the writing of royal inscriptions ... that potential was unrealised').

33. Sancisi-Weerdenburg 2001a: 337; for comparison with Rome, cf. Dusinberre 2003: 203-16.

34. Briant 2002: 868.

35. It is impossible to speculate with any authority on the relationship between the Islamic revolution and increased western interest in Iranian history. Root, 2002: i, observes that 'perversely enough' North American and European scholarship has thrived during a 'prolonged era of virtual isolation of U.S. citizens from Iran'. Could it be that the birth of the Islamic Republic gave Iranian history a peculiar mystique, or that (as with some nineteenth-century writers, discussed above, Chapter 5) it prompted interest as a way of reaching over the heads of contemporary Iranians to their ancient predecessors?

36. Not least Hall 1989.

37. Said 1978: e.g. 11, 20-1.

38. Sancisi-Weerdenburg 1987c: 130 (for adoption of Said, see esp. 117-18); for Ctesias' invention of Orient, Sancisi-Weerdenburg 1987b (but see now the corrective of Lenfant 2004: cxxxvi). The rather passing use of 'Orientalism' as a charter for the new Achaemenid historiography is exemplified by Dusinberre's reference: 2003: 9n.35. See also here the observations of Vasunia 2003: 88-9 on the appropriation of Said in the context of Hellenism.

39. E.g. Kuhrt 1995: 648, quoted above, ch. 3, Briant 2002: 268 on 'Orientalising' stereotypes. See now the passing description by Henkelman 2008: 62 of Walther Hinz and Heidemarie Koch as 'Orientalist'.

40. Root 2003: 3; see also Root 2008: 195-6, imagining an excessive 'commonality of ethos' regarding Persia in western scholarship.

41. Thomas 2000.

42. Miller 1997: 1; for artistic representations of non-Greeks, see also Cohen 2000.

43. For accounts of the impact of Persia on the Greek world and Greek ideas, see Rhodes 2007, Marincola 2007; for a nuanced survey of Athenian representations of Persia, Tuplin 1996: 132-77.

44. Waldemar Januszczak (*Sunday Times, Culture*, 11 Sept. 2005, p. 8); cf. Saïd 2002 on Euripides.

45. See further Harrison 2007.

46. Contrast Miller's focus, 1997, on 'marginalisation' as a way of containing the threat posed by Persian borrowings while allowing them to become new weapons in the inter-aristocratic battle for prestige.

47. Lloyd, in discussion of Briant 1990 (p. 109): mercenaries 'might acquire their 200 words or so of Persian and be perfectly fluent when dealing with a closed context like the drill yard or selling onions, but this does not mean that they would be capable of dealing with Iranian theology or of extracting detailed information on the organisation of the army ...'. I do not mean to suggest that there may not have been some Greeks whose grasp of

Persian language (and even of Iranian theology!) might have been more advanced.

48. This complex, multilayered relationship is well brought out by Vasunia 2007, esp. 228-9.

49. Moyer 2002; cf. Rollinger 2000, Dillery 2005.

50. Munson 2009: 463 (I am doubtful of her extreme emphasis on Herodotus' reflection of dissenting Persian voices); cf. West 2003, Luraghi's observations on Herodotus' presentation of the plurality of Persian traditions, 2001: 155-6, and now (from a different perspective) Waters 2010: 65 on Cyrus' upbringing at Astyages' court.

51. Haubold 2007: 4; see also now Root 2007: 178-9, Kim 2009: 26-9, suggesting that the Persian sense of a unitary Greek world may have informed Panhellenist ideas. For Persian characterisations of the Greek world see Sancisi-Weerdenburg 2001b, Kuhrt 2002, Rollinger 2006.

52. Lenfant 2001; see also Lenfant 2007 (on Athenaeus' role in developing the theme of luxury), Tuplin 2007: xvi, Tuplin 1996 (esp. 149-50, 162, 169-70), concluding (p. 176) that 'there was too widespread a connivance in low level imitation of Persian *trûphê* for anyone to have much interest in denouncing it ...'. Contrast Briant's hardening of the theme of luxury into a 'theory of "Persian decadence"', 2002: 787.

53. See e.g. the formulation of Sancisi-Weerdenburg 2001a: 340.

54. See e.g. Briant's account of the landscape of scholarship on Achaemenid history, 2001: 'To speak bluntly, what is really *new* in what is published recently? In our domain, what are the signs that permit us to assert that this or that study marks *progress* in the order of knowledge? The answer may seem easy as long as one is dealing with publications of documents, but it is quite a different matter when one considers interpretative publications.' Davidson 2006: 35 caricatures Briant 2002 as a 'recent document-stuffed study of another Greek Other'.

55. Brosius 2006b: 430 on Briant 2003a, citing Woodman 1988, Hartog 1988 and Griffiths 1989 as 'operat[ing] along the same lines as Briant'.

56. Sancisi-Weerdenburg 1983: 32. Brosius' description, 1996: 195, of the three different factors which informed Greek accounts likewise has the effect of marginalising Greek sources beyond all reasonable limits.

57. Political thought: Sancisi-Weerdenburg 1993b: 145-6. Foreign policy: Wiesehofer 2004.

58. Wiesehöfer 2004: 212, criticising Harrison 2002: 577 ('the image of the king's lust for revenge and world domination – both actual features of Persian court ideology'); I had not intended to suggest, in a very condensed formulation, that the relationship of 'actual' Persian ideology and Greek image was anything other than distant and partial. For a contrasting view of a Persian ideology of world conquest, see Tuplin 1991: 278-9, Cawkwell 2005: 49, 66; for Persia as a model of imperial expansion for National Socialism, Wiesehöfer 1988.

59. Cf. Briant 2002: 158.

60. DB 1.20-24; cf. DB 4.61-7 ('The man who cooperated with my house, him I rewarded well; whoso did injury, him I punished well').

61. DNb 16-21.

62. Herodotus 6.9; cf. 1.114-15, the story of the boy Cyrus' punishment of Artembares' son (if you don't do what the King orders, you get whipped).

63. Sancisi-Weerdenburg 1999: 98.

64. Root 1990: 116 in the context of the symbolism of Persepolis.

65. I am grateful to Kostas Vlassopoulos for stiffening my thinking here. Contrast, however, Briant 1989a.

66. Bridges, Hall and Rhodes 2007: 12; cf. Bowden 1998: 110, Vasunia 2003: 89.

67. Hanson 2007: 3.

68. Holland 2005.

69. Pagden 2008: xxi.

70. See here Marchand 2009: xxi, Lianieri 2007: esp. 336, citing Vasunia 2003: 89: 'To trace the roots of Orientalism back to Greece ..., while assuming, simultaneously, a continuity between antiquity and modernity, is to bestow on the Greek past a sanctity of origin and ignore how that sanctity was founded on self-legitimation, denial and violence.'

71. For example, Aristagoras of Miletus' boasting of his relationship with Artaphernes, Herodotus 5.30.

72. Herodotus 1.134; cf. Briant 2002: 200-3, 310-12, Harrison 2009.

73. Herodotus 2.158, reflected at Meiggs and Lewis 1988: no. 7a.

74. See further Vasunia 2001.

75. Strauss and Ober 1990: 105-6 ('It took talent on A's part to win; it also took errors on Persia's part to lose').

76. See further Harrison 2002.

77. A model encapsulated in Vernant 1962 ('Avènement de la Polis, naissance de la philosophie', p. 131).

78. Pagden 2008: 30.

79. Hanson 2007: 3.

80. 'The sturdy infant [democracy] nestled under the protecting aegis of a "barbarian" monarchy' (Olmstead 1938: 311). See e.g. Herodotus 6.42-3 for the measures taken after the Ionian revolt, with Briant 2002: 493-7 (concluding, p. 496, that 'these measures did away with some of the systemic dysfunctionality' that had contributed to the revolt), Wiesehöfer 2004: 216-18 for a plausible reconstruction of 'Persian plans for a conquered Hellas', Georges 2000 for an argument that pre-revolt Ionia had prospered under Persian rule. Weiskopf 2008 casts doubt on the post-revolt settlement, attributing Herodotus' account to 'imperial nostalgia'.

81. For the size of Greek cities, see e.g. Price and Nixon 1990, Hansen 2006: 73-6. Cf. Austin 1990: 295-6, questioning how much difference the change from Lydians to Persians would have made for Greeks of Asia Minor. See also the balanced observations of Bowden 1998: 110; cf. Young 1980: 238.

82. See e.g. DSe 30-4, DNa 32, DNb 16-21; Herodotus 5.49, 7.9.b1-2. For an exhaustive account of the field of reference of 'medism' and for a comparison of Persian/Greek elite lifestyle, see Tuplin 1997a.

83. D.M. Lewis 1977: 158.

Bibliography

Abdi, K. (2010) 'The passing of the throne from Xerxes to Artaxerxes I, or how an archaeological observation can be a potential contribution to Achaemenid historiography', in J. Curtis and St.-J. Simpson (eds) *The World of Achaemenid Persia: History, Art and Society in Iran and the Ancient Near East* (London), 275-84.

Ackroyd, P.R. (1990) 'The biblical portrayal of Achaemenid rulers', in H. Sancisi-Weerdenburg and J.W. Drijvers (eds) *Achaemenid History V: The Roots of the European Tradition* (Leiden), 1-16.

Ahn, G. (1992) *Religiöse Herrscherlegitimation im Achaemenidischen Iran: Die Voraussetzungen und die Struktur ihrer Argumentation* (Leiden and Louvain).

Allen, L. (2005a) *The Persian Empire: A History* (London).

Allen, L. (2005b) '*Le roi imaginaire*: an audience with the Achaemenid king', in O. Hekster and R. Fowler (eds) *Imaginary Kings: The Royal Image in the Ancient Near East* (Oriens et Occidens 11, Stuttgart), 39-62.

Allen, L. (2007) '"Chilminar *olim* Persepolis": European receptions of a Persian ruin', in C.J. Tuplin (ed.) *Persian Responses: Political and Cultural Interaction with(in) the Achaemenid Empire* (Swansea), 313-42.

Amory Jr., C. (1929) *Persian Days* (Boston and New York).

Anderson, T.S. (1880) *My Wanderings in Persia* (London).

Andrewes, A. (1956) *The Greek Tyrants* (London).

Aperghis, G.G. (1997) 'Surplus, exchange and price in the Persepolis fortification texts', in J. Andreau, P. Briant and R. Descat (eds) *Économie Antique. Prix et formation des prix dans les economies antiques* (St-Bertrand-de-Comminges), 277-90.

Aperghis, G.G. (2000) 'War captives and economic exploitation: evidence from the Persepolis Fortification Tablets', in J. Andreau, P. Briant, R. Descat (eds) *Économie Antique. La guerre dans les économies antiques* (St-Bertrand-de-Comminges), 127-44.

Armayor, O.K. (1978) 'Herodotus' catalogues of the Persian Empire in the light of the monuments and the Greek literary tradition', *Transactions of the American Philological Association* 108, 1-9.

Arnold, A. (1877) *Through Persia by Caravan* (New York).

Bibliography

Asheri, D. (1999) 'Erodoto e Bisitun', in E. Gabba (ed.) *Presentazione e Scrittura della Storia: Storiografia, Epigrafi, Monumenti* (Como), 101-16.

Austin, M.M. (1990) 'Greek tyrants and the Persians 546-479 BC', *Classical Quarterly* 40 (1990), 289-306.

Austin, M.M. (2003) 'The Seleukids and Asia'. in A. Erskine (ed.) *A Companion to the Hellenistic World* (Oxford), 121-33.

Badian, E. (1985) 'Alexander in Iran', in I. Gershevitch (ed.) *Cambridge History of Iran*, vol. 2: *The Median and Achaemenian periods* (Cambridge), 420-501.

Baines, J. (1996) 'On the composition and inscriptions of the Vatican statue of Udjahorresnet', in P. De Manuelian (ed.) *Studies in Honor of W.K. Simpson I* (Boston), 83-92.

Baker, H.D. (2008) 'Babylon in 484 BC: the excavated archival tablets as a source for urban history', *Zeitschrift für Assyriologie* 98, 100-16.

Baker, V. (1876) *Clouds in the East: Travels and Adventures on the Perso-Turkoman Frontier* (London).

Balcer, J.M. (1978) 'Alexander's burning of Persepolis', *Iranica Antiqua* 13, 119-33.

Balcer, J.M. (1987) *Herodotus and Bisitun: Problems in Ancient Persian Historiography* (Stuttgart).

Balcer, J.M. (1989) 'The Persian wars against Greece: a reassessment', *Historia* 38, 127-43.

Balcer, J.M. (1995) *The Persian Conquest of the Greeks 545-450 BC* (Konstanz).

Bassett, J. (1886) *Persia: The Land of the Imams. A Narrative of Travel and Residence 1871-1885* (New York).

Bedford, P.R. (2007) 'The Persian Near East', in W. Scheidel, I. Morris, R.P. Saller (eds) *Cambridge Economic History of the Greco-Roman World* (Cambridge), 302-29.

Bell, G. (1928) *Persian Pictures* (London, with introduction by E. Denison Ross; originally published anonymously as *Safar Nameh. Persian Pictures. A Book of Travel*, 1898).

Benjamin, S.G.W. (1887) *Persia and the Persians* (Boston).

Berenson, B. (1954) *Aesthetics and History* (Garden City NY).

Bickermann, E.J. (1963) 'À propos d'un passage de Chares de Mytilène', *Parola del Passato* 91, 241-55.

Bigwood, J.M. (1978) 'Ctesias as historian of the Persian wars', *Phoenix* 32, 19-41.

Boardman, J. (1964) *The Greeks Overseas* (London).

Boardman, J. (2000) *Persia and the West: An Archaeological Investigation of the Genesis of Achaemenid Art* (London).

Boedeker, D. (1988) 'Protesilaos and the end of Herodotus' *Histories*', *Classical Antiquity* 7, 30-48.

Bosworth, A.B. (1996) *Alexander and the East: The Tragedy of Triumph* (Oxford).

Bibliography

Bosworth, C.E. (1993) 'The Hon. George Nathaniel Curzon's travels in Russian central Asia and Persia', *Iran* 31, 127-36.

Bosworth, C.E. (1995) 'E.G. Browne and his *A Year Amongst the Persians*', *Iran* 33, 115-22.

Bovon, A. (1963) 'La représentation des guerriers perses et la notion de Barbare dans la première moitié du Ve siècle', *Bulletin du Correspondance Héllenique* 87, 579-602.

Bowden, H. (1998) 'Great and wonderful deeds: the changing historiography of the Persian wars', *Dialogos. Hellenic Studies Review* 5, 101-10.

Bradley-Birt, F.B. (1909) *Through Persia: From the Gulf to the Caspian* (London).

Brentjes, B. (1995) 'The history of Elam and Achaemenid Persia: an overview', in J. Sasson (with J. Baines, G. Beckman, K.S. Robinson) (eds) *Civilisations of the Ancient Near East* (New York), 2.1001-21.

Briant, P. (1979a) 'Des Achéménides aux rois hellenistiques: continuités et ruptures', *Annali della Scuola Normale di Pisa* 6, 1375-414, reprinted as Briant (1982), 291-330.

Briant, P. (1979b) 'Impérialismes antiques et idéologie coloniale dans la France contemporaine: Alexandre le Grand modèle colonial', *Dialogues d'Histoire Ancienne* 5, 283-92, reprinted as Briant (1982), 281-92.

Briant, P. (1980) 'Conquête territorial et stratégie idéologique: Alexandre le Grand et l'idéologie monarchique achéménide', in *L'idéologie monarchique dans l'Antiquité* (Actes du colloque international sur l'idéologie monarchique dans l'antiquité, Cracovie-Mogilany du 23 au 26 octobre 1977), vol. 63, 37-83, reprinted as Briant (1982), 357-403.

Briant, P. (1982) *Rois, tributs et paysans: études sur les formations tributaires du moyen-orient ancien* (Paris).

Briant, P. (1988) 'Ethno-classe dominante et populations soumises dans l'empire achéménide: le cas de l'Égypte', in A. Kuhrt and H. Sancisi-Weerdenburg (eds) *Achaemenid History III: Method and Theory* (Leiden) 137-73.

Briant, P. (1989a) 'Histoire et idéologie. Les Grecs et la décadence Perse', in M.-M. Mactoux and E. Geny (eds) *Mélanges P. Lévêque*, vol. II: *Anthropologie et Société* (Besançon), 33-47, translated as 'History as ideology: the Greeks and "Persian" decadence', in T. Harrison (ed.) *Greeks and Barbarians* (Edinburgh, 2002), 193-210.

Briant, P. (1989b) 'Table du roi. Tribut et redistribution chez les Achéménides', in P. Briant and C. Herrenschmidt (eds) *Le tribut dans l'empire perse* (Paris), 35-44.

Briant, P. (1990) 'Hérodote et la société perse', in W. Burkert et al., *Hérodote et les peuples non-Grecs*, Entretiens Hardt 35 (Geneva), 69-113.

Briant, P. (1994a) 'L'eau du grand roi', in L. Milano (ed.) *Drinking in Ancient Societies* (Padua), 45-65.

Briant, P. (1994b) 'L'histoire achéménide: sources, methodes, raissonements et modèles', *Topoi Orient-Occident* 4, 109-30.

Bibliography

Briant, P. (1996) *Alexander the Great: The Heroic Ideal* (London); tr. J. Leggatt from French original, *Alexandre le Grand* (Paris, 1987).

Briant, P. (1999), 'L'histoire de l'empire achéménide aujourd'hui: l'historien et ses documents', *Annales HSS* 54.5, 1127-36.

Briant, P. (2001) 'New trends in Achaemenid history' (Noruz Lecture, Foundation for Iranian Studies, Washington DC, 23 March 2001), *Iran Nameh* 18.4, also available at http://www.cais-soas.com/CAIS/History/hakhamaneshian/new_trends.htm, revised version published in *Ancient History Bulletin* 17 (2003), 33-47.

Briant, P. (2002) *From Cyrus to Alexander: A History of the Persian Empire*, tr. Peter T. Daniels (Lake Winona); originally published as *Histoire de l'Empire Perse de Cyrus à Alexandre* (Paris, 1996).

Briant, P. (2003a) *Darius dans l'ombre d'Alexandre* (Paris).

Briant, P. (2003b) 'Histoire et archéologie d'un texte: la *Lettre de Darius à Gadatas* entre Perses, Grecs et Romains', in M. Giorgieri, M. Salvini, M-C. Trémouille and P. Vannicelli (eds) *Licia e Lidia prima dell' ellenizzazione* (Rome), 107-44.

Briant, P. (2005) 'Milestones in the development of Achaemenid historiography in the era of Ernst Herzfeld', in A.C. Gunter and S. Hauser (eds) (2005) *Ernst Herzfeld and the Development of Near Eastern Studies 1900-1950* (Leiden), 263-80.

Briant, P. (2008) *Lettre ouverte à Alexandre le grand* (Paris).

Briant, P. (2009a) 'The empire of Darius III in perspective', in W. Heckel and L.A. Tritle (eds) *Alexander the Great: A New History* (Chichester, Malden MA, Oxford), 141-70.

Briant, P. (2009b) 'Alexander and the Persian empire, between "decline" and "renovation" ', in W. Heckel and L.A. Tritle (eds) *Alexander the Great: A New History* (Chichester, Malden MA, Oxford), 171-88.

Briant, P. and R. Boucharlat (eds) (2005) *L'archéologie de l'empire achémémide: nouvelles recherches* (Persika 6, Paris).

Briant, P. and F. Joannès (eds) (2006) *La transition entre l'empire achéménide et les royaumes hellénistiques* (Persika 9, Paris).

Bridges, E., E. Hall and P.J. Rhodes (2007) 'Introduction', in E. Bridges, E. Hall and P.J. Rhodes (eds) *Cultural Responses to the Persian Wars: Antiquity to the Third Millennium* (Oxford), 3-29.

Brosius, M. (1990) 'Two views on Persian history in eighteenth century England', in H. Sancisi-Weerdenburg and J.W. Drijvers (eds) *Achaemenid History V: The Roots of the European Tradition* (Leiden), 79-89.

Brosius, M. (1996) *Women in Ancient Persia (559-331 BC)* (Oxford).

Brosius, M. (2000) *The Persian Empire from Cyrus II to Artaxerxes I* (LACTOR 16, London).

Brosius, M. (2003a) 'Alexander and the Persians', in J. Roisman (ed.) *Brill's Companion to Alexander the Great* (Leiden), 169-93.

Brosius, M. (2003b) 'Why Persia became the enemy of Macedon', in W. Henkelman and A. Kuhrt (eds) *Achaemenid History XIII: A Persian*

Perspective. Essays in Memory of Heleen Sancisi-Weerdenburg (Leiden), 227-37.

Brosius, M. (2003c) 'Reconstructing an archive: account and journal texts from Persepolis', in M. Brosius (ed.) *Ancient Archives and Archival Traditions: Concepts of Record-Keeping in the Ancient World* (Oxford), 264-83.

Brosius, M. (2005) '*Pax persica*: Königliche Ideologie und Kriegführung im Achämenidenreich', in B. Meissner, O. Schmitt, M. Sommer (eds) *Krieg – Gesellschaft – Institutionen: Beiträge zu einer vergleichenden Kriegsgeschichte* (Stuttgart), 135-61.

Brosius, M. (2006a) *The Persians: An Introduction* (London).

Brosius, M. (2006b) review of Briant 2003a, *Gnomon* 78, 426-30.

Brosius, M. (2007) 'New out of old? Court and court ceremonies in Achaemenid Persia', in A.J.S. Spawforth (ed.) *The Court and Court Society in Ancient Monarchies* (Cambridge), 17-57.

Brosius, M. (2010) 'The royal audience scene reconsidered', in J. Curtis and St.-J. Simpson (eds) *The World of Achaemenid Persia: History, Art and Society in Iran and the Ancient Near East* (London), 141-52.

Browne, E.G. (1926) *A Year Amongst the Persians. Impressions as to the life, character and thought of the people of Persia. Received during twelve months' residence in that country in the years 1887-1888 by EGB. With a memoir by Sir E. Denison Ross* (Cambridge, original publication 1893).

Burgess, C. and E. (1942) *Letters from Persia. Written by Charles and Edward Burgess 1828-1855*, edited by Benjamin Schwartz (New York).

Cameron, G.G. (1936) *History of Early Iran* (Chicago).

Cameron, G.G. (1948) *Persepolis Treasury Tablets* (Chicago).

Carroll, M. (1960) *From a Persian Tea-house* (London).

Casson, S. (1938) 'Achaemenid sculpture', in A.U. Pope (ed.) *A Survey of Persian Art: From Prehistoric Times to the Present*, vol. 1 (London and New York), 346-66.

Cawkwell, G. (2005) *The Greek Wars: The Failure of Persia* (Oxford).

Cohen, B. (2000), *Not the Classical Ideal: Athens and the Construction of the Other in Greek Art* (Leiden).

Collins, E.T. (1896) *In the Kingdom of the Shah. The Journey of a Medical Man through Persia* (London).

Connor, W.R. (1987) 'Tribes, festivals and processions: civic ceremonial and political manipulation in Archaic Greece', *Journal of Hellenic Studies* 107, 40-50.

Cook, J.M. (1962) *The Greeks in Ionia and the East* (London).

Cook, J.M. (1983) *The Persian Empire* (London).

Cook, J.M. (1985) 'The rise of the Achaemenids and the establishment of their empire', in I. Gershevitch (ed.) *Cambridge History of Iran*, vol. 2: *The Median and Achaemenian periods* (Cambridge), 200-91.

Cooke, R.S. (1938) 'Achaemenid seals C. Aesthetic character', in A.U. Pope (ed.) *A Survey of Persian Art: From Prehistoric Times to the Present*, vol. 1 (London and New York), 394-6.

Bibliography

Cruz-Uribe, E. (2003) 'The invasion of Egypt by Cambyses', *Transeuphratène* 25, 9-60.

Curtis, J. and N. Tallis (eds) (2005) *Forgotten Empire: The World of Ancient Persia* (London).

Curzon, G. (1892) *Persia and the Persian Question* (London & New York).

Davidson, J.N. (2006) 'Making a spectacle of her(self): the Greek courtesan and the art of the present', in M. Feldman and B. Gordon (eds) *The Courtesan's Arts: Cross-cultural Perspectives* (New York), 29-51.

de Lorey, E. and D. Sladen (1907) *Queer Things about Persia* (London).

de Windt, H. (1891) *A Ride to India across Persia and Baluchistan* (London).

Depuydt, L. (1995) 'Murder in Memphis: the story of Cambyses' mortal wounding of the Apis bull (c.a. 523 BCE)', *Journal of Near Eastern Studies* 54, 119-26.

Desmond, W. (2004) 'Punishments and the conclusion of Herodotus' Histories', *Greek, Roman, and Byzantine Studies* 44, 19-40.

Devauchelle, D. (1995) 'Le sentiment anti-perse chez les anciens Égyptiens', *Transeuphratène* 9', 67-80.

Devauchelle, D. (1998) 'Une problem de chronologie sous Cambyse', *Transeuphratène* 15, 9-17.

Dewald, C. (1997) 'Wanton kings, picked heroes, and gnomic founding fathers: strategies of meaning at the end of Herodotus' *Histories*', in D.H. Roberts, F.M. Dunn, and D. Fowler (eds) *Classical Closure* (Princeton), 62-82.

Dillery, J. (2005) 'Cambyses and the Egyptian *Chaosbeschreibung* tradition', *Classical Quarterly* 55, 387-406.

Duchesne-Guillemin, J. (1972) 'La religion des Achéménides', in G. Walser (ed.) *Beiträge zur Achämenidengeschichte* (Stuttgart), 59-82.

Durand, E.R. (1902) *An Autumn Tour in Western Persia* (London).

Dusinberre, E.R.M. (2003) *Aspects of Empire in Achaemenid Sardis* (Cambridge).

Eastwick, E. (1864) *Three Year's Residence in Persia* (London).

Fehling, D. (1989) *Herodotus and his 'Sources': Citation, Invention and Narrative Art,* tr. J.G. Howie (Leeds).

Flower, M. (2000) 'Alexander the Great and Panhellenism', in A.B. Bosworth and E.J. Baynham (eds) *Alexander the Great in Fact and Fiction* (Oxford), 96-135.

Forrest, W.G. (1979) 'Motivation in Herodotos: the case of the Ionian revolt', *International History Review* 1, 311-22.

Fowler, G. (1841) *Three Years in Persia; with travelling adventures in Koordistan* (London).

Fowler, R. (1996) 'Herodotus and his contemporaries', *Journal of Hellenic Studies* 116, 62-87.

Frankfort, H. (1946) 'Achaemenian sculpture', *American Journal of Archaeology* 50 (1946), 6-14.

Fredricksmeyer, E. (2000) 'Alexander the Great and the Kingship of Asia', in A.B. Bosworth and E.J. Baynham (eds) *Alexander the Great in Fact and Fiction* (Oxford), 136-66.

Fromkin, D. (1991) 'The importance of T.E. Lawrence', *New Criterion* 10 (Sept.), http://www.newcriterion.com/archive/10/sept91/fromkin.htm

Frye, R. (1983) *The History of Ancient Iran* (Munich).

Garvin, E.E. (2003) 'Darius III and Homeland Defense', in W. Heckel and L. Tritle (eds) *Crossroads of History* (Claremont CA), 87-111.

Gates, J. (2003) 'The ethnicity name game: what lies behind "Graeco-Persian"?', in M.C. Root (ed.) *Medes and Persians: Reflections on Elusive Empires. Ars Orientalis* 32 (2002), 105-32.

George, A.R. (2010) 'Xerxes and the tower of Babel', in J. Curtis and St.-J. Simpson (eds) *The World of Achaemenid Persia: History, Art and Society in Iran and the Ancient Near East* (London), 471-80.

Georges, P.B. (2000) 'Persian Ionia under Darius: the revolt reconsidered', *Historia* 49, 1-39.

Gera, D.L. (1993) *Xenophon's* Cyropaedia*: Style, Genre and Literary Technique* (Oxford).

Gikandi, S. (1996) *Maps of Englishness: Writing Identity in the Culture of Colonialism* (New York).

Gopnik, H. (2010) 'Why columned halls?', in J. Curtis and St.-J. Simpson (eds) *The World of Achaemenid Persia: History, Art and Society in Iran and the Ancient Near East* (London), 195-206.

Graf, D.F. (1985) 'Greek tyrants and Achaemenid politics', in J.W. Eadie and J. Ober (eds) *The Craft of the Ancient Historian: Essays in Honor of Chester G. Starr* (Lanham MD), 79-123.

Graves, R. (1948) *Collected Poems 1914-1947* (London)

Green, P. (1996) *The Greco-Persian Wars* (Berkeley).

Griffiths, A. (1987). 'Democedes of Croton: a Greek doctor at the court of Darius', in H. Sancisi-Weerdenburg and A. Kuhrt (eds) *Achaemenid History II: The Greek Sources* (Leiden), 37-51.

Griffiths, A. (1989) 'Was Cleomenes mad?' in A. Powell (ed.) *Classical Sparta: Techniques behind her Success* (London), 51-78.

Griffiths, A. (1999) 'Euenius the negligent nightwatchman (Herodotus 9.92-6)', in R. Buxton (ed.) *From Myth to Reason? Essays in the Development of Greek Thought* (Oxford), 169-82.

Griffiths, A. (2001) 'Kissing cousins: some curious cases of adjacent material in Herodotus', in N. Luraghi (ed.) *The Historian's Craft in the Age of Herodotus* (Oxford), 161-78.

Gruen, E. (2005) 'Persia through the Jewish looking-glass', in E.S. Gruen (ed.) *Cultural Borrowings and Ethnic Appropriations in Antiquity* (Oriens et Occidens 8, Stuttgart), 90-104.

Grundy, G.B. (1901) *The Great Persian War and its Preliminaries: A Study of the Evidence, Literary and Topographical* (London).

Gunter, A.C. (1990) 'Models of the Orient in the art history of the Orientalizing period', in H. Sancisi-Weerdenburg and J.W. Drijvers (eds)

Bibliography

Achaemenid History V: The Roots of the European Tradition (Leiden), 130-47.

Gunter, A.C. (2009) *Greek Art and the Orient* (Cambridge).

Gunter, A.C. and S. Hauser (2005) 'Ernst Herzfeld and Near Eastern Studies, 1900-1950', in A.C. Gunter and S. Hauser (eds) *Ernst Herzfeld and the Development of Near Eastern Studies 1900-1950* (Leiden), 3-39.

Hall, E. (1989) *Inventing the Barbarian: Greek Self-Definition through Tragedy* (Oxford).

Hallock, R.T. (1969) *Persepolis Fortification Tablets* (Chicago).

Hallock, R.T. (1971) *The Evidence of the Persepolis Tablets* (Cambridge).

Hallock, R.T. (1973) 'The Persepolis fortification archive', *Orientalia* 42, 320-3.

Hammond, N.G.L. (1996) 'The construction of Xerxes' bridge over the Hellespont', *Journal of Hellenic Studies* 116, 88-107.

Hansen, M.H. (2006) *Polis: An Introduction to the Ancient Greek City-State* (Oxford).

Hanson, V.D. (2007) 'Persian versions', *Times Literary Supplement*, 18 May 2007, 3-4.

Harrison, T. (2000) *The Emptiness of Asia: Aeschylus' Persians and the History of the Fifth Century* (London).

Harrison, T. (2002) 'The Persian invasions', in E. Bakker, I. De Jong and H. Van Wees (eds) *Brill's Companion to Herodotus* (Leiden), 551-78.

Harrison, T. (2003a) 'Prophecy in reverse: Herodotus and the origins of history', in P.S. Derow and R. Parker (eds) *Herodotus and his World: Essays from a Conference in Memory of George Forrest* (Oxford), 237-55.

Harrison, T. (2003b) 'Upside down and back to front: Herodotus and the Greek encounter with Egypt', in R. Matthews and C. Roemer (eds) *Ancient Perspectives on Egypt* (London), 145-55.

Harrison, T. (2004) 'Truth and lies in Herodotus' *Histories*', in I. Taifacos and V. Karageorghis (eds) *The World of Herodotus* (Nicosia), 255-63.

Harrison, T. (2007) 'The place of geography in Herodotus' *Histories*', in C. Adams and J. Roy (eds) *Travel, Geography and Culture in Ancient Greece, Egypt, and the Near East* (Oxford), 44-65.

Harrison, T. (2008) 'Ancient and modern imperialism', *Greece and Rome* 55, 1-22.

Harrison, T. (2009) 'Oliver Stone, *Alexander*, and the unity of mankind', in P. Cartledge and F. Rose Greenland (eds) *Responses to Oliver Stone's Alexander: Film, History, and Cultural Studies* (Madison WI), 219-42.

Hartog, F. (1988) *The Mirror of Herodotus: The Representation of the Other in the Writing of History*, tr. J. Lloyd (Berkeley).

Haubold, J. (2007) 'Xerxes' Homer', in E. Bridges, E. Hall and P.J. Rhodes (eds) *Cultural Responses to the Persian Wars: Antiquity to the Third Millennium* (Oxford), 47-62.

Henkelman, W. (2008) *The Other Gods who Are: Studies in Elamite-Iranian*

Bibliography

Acculturation Based on the Persepolis Fortification Texts, Achaemenid History XIV (Leiden).

Henkelman, W. (forthcoming) ' "Consumed before the King": the Table of Darius, that of Irdabama and Irtaštuna, and that of his satrap, Karkiš', in B. Jacobs & R. Rollinger (eds), *Der Achämenidenhof* (Oriens et Occidens, Stuttgart).

Herzfeld, E. (1935) *Archaeological History of Iran* (London).

Herzfeld, E. (1941) *Iran in the Ancient East. Archaeological Studies presented in the Lowell Lectures at Boston* (Oxford).

Holland, T. (2005) *Persian Fire: The First World Empire and the Battle for the West* (London).

Holm-Rasmussen, T. (1988) 'Collaboration in early Achaemenid Egypt: a new approach', in A. Damsgaard-Madsen, E. Christiansen and E. Hallager (eds) *Studies in Ancient History and Numismatics presented to Rudi Thomsen* (Aarhus), 29-38.

Hopkins, K. (1963) 'Eunuchs in politics in the later Roman empire', *Proceedings of the Cambridge Philological Society* 189, 62-80.

Hornblower, S. (1990) 'Achaemenid history' (review of *Achaemenid History I-III*), *Classical Review* 40, 89-95.

Irwin, E. and E. Greenwood (2007) 'Introduction', in E. Irwin and E. Greenwood (eds) *Reading Herodotus: A Study of the* Logoi *in Book 5 for Herodotus'* Histories (Cambridge), 1-40.

Jackson, A.V.W. (1906) *Persia Past and Present: A Book of Travel and Research* (New York)

Jacobs, B. (2010) 'From gabled hut to rock-cut tomb: a religious and cultural break between Cyrus and Darius', in J. Curtis and St.-J. Simpson (eds) *The World of Achaemenid Persia: History, Art and Society in Iran and the Ancient Near East* (London), 91-101.

Jamzadeh, P. (1995) 'Darius' thrones: temporal and eternal', *Iranica Antiqua* 30, 1-21.

Joisten-Pruschke, A. (2010) 'Light from Aramaic documents', in J. Curtis and St.-J. Simpson (eds) *The World of Achaemenid Persia: History, Art and Society in Iran and the Ancient Near East* (London), 41-9.

Jones, C.E. and M. Stolper (2008) 'How many Persepolis Fortification tablets are there?', in P. Briant, W. Henkelman and M. Stolper (eds) *L'archive des Fortifications de Persépolis: état des questions et perspectives de recherches* (Persika 12, Paris), 27-50.

Kaptan, D. (2002) *The Daskyleion Bullae: Seal Images from the Western Achaemenid Empire, Achaemenid History XII* (2 vols, Leiden).

Katouzian, H. (2009) *The Persians: Ancient, Mediaeval and Modern Iran* (New Haven).

Kawami, T.S. (1986) 'Greek art and Persian taste: some animal sculptures from Persepolis', *American Journal of Archaeology* 90, 259-67.

Kellens, J. (1969) 'Sur un parallèle inverse à l'inscription des "daiva"', *Studi e materiali di storia delle religioni* 40, 209-13.

171

Bibliography

Kellens, J. (2002) 'L'idéologie religieuse des inscriptions achéménides', *Journal Asiatique* 290, 417-64.

Kent, R.G. (1953) *Old Persian: Grammar, Texts, Lexicon* (2nd edn, New Haven).

Keaveney, A. (1996) 'Persian behaviour and misbehaviour: some Herodotean examples', *Athenaeum* 84, 23-48.

Kim, H.J. (2009) *Ethnicity and Foreigners in Ancient Greece and China* (London).

Kinneir, J. Macdonald (1813) *A Geographical Memoir of the Persian Empire, accompanied by a map* (London).

Klinkott, H. (2005) *Der Satrap. Ein Achaimenidischer Amsträger und seine Handlungsspielraüme* (Frankfurt am Main).

Kuhrt, A. (1983) 'The Cyrus Cylinder and Achaemenid imperial policy', *Journal for the Study of the Old Testament* 25, 83-97.

Kuhrt, A. (1987) 'Usurpation, conquest and ceremonial: from Babylon to Persia', in D. Cannadine and S. Price (eds) *Rituals of Royalty: Power and Ceremonial in Traditional Societies* (Cambridge), 20-55.

Kuhrt, A. (1990) 'Alexander and Babylon', in H. Sancisi-Weerdenburg and J.W. Drijvers (eds) *Achaemenid History V: The Roots of the European Tradition* (Leiden), 121-30.

Kuhrt, A. (1995) *The Ancient Near East c. 3000-300 BC* (2 vols, London).

Kuhrt, A. (1997) 'Some thoughts on P. Briant, *Histoire de l'empire perse*', *Topoi* Supplement 1, 299-304.

Kuhrt, A. (2001) 'The Persian kings and their subjects: a unique relationship' (review of P. Frei and K. Koch, *Reichsidee und Reichsorganisation im Perserreich*, Göttingen 1996), *Orientalistische Literaturzeitung* 96/2, 167-73.

Kuhrt, A. (2002) *'Greeks' and 'Greek' in Mesopotamian and Persian Perspectives. The Twenty-first J.L. Myres Memorial Lecture* (Oxford).

Kuhrt, A. (2003) 'Making history: Sargon of Agade and Cyrus the Great of Persia', in W. Henkelman and A. Kuhrt (eds) *Achaemenid History XIII: A Persian Perspective. Essays in Memory of Heleen Sancisi-Weerdenburg* (Leiden), 347-61.

Kuhrt, A. (2007) *The Persian Empire: A Corpus of Sources from the Achaemenid Period* (2 vols, London).

Kuhrt, A. (2009) 'Heleen Sancisi-Weerdenburg', *Encyclopaedia Iranica Online*, www.iranica.com.

Kuhrt, A. (2010) 'Xerxes and the Babylonian temples: a restatement of the case', in J. Curtis and St.-J. Simpson (eds) *The World of Achaemenid Persia: History, Art and Society in Iran and the Ancient Near East* (London), 491-4.

Kuhrt, A. and H. Sancisi-Weerdenburg (1987) 'Introduction', in H. Sancisi-Weerdenburg and A. Kuhrt (eds) *Achaemenid History II: The Greek Sources* (Leiden), ix-xiii.

Kuhrt, A. and S. Sherwin-White (1987) 'Xerxes destruction of Babylonian temples', in H. Sancisi-Weerdenburg and A. Kuhrt (eds) *Achaemenid History II: The Greek Sources* (Leiden), 69-78.

Kurke, L. (1999) *Coins, Bodies, Games, and Gold: The Politics of Meaning in Archaic Greece* (Princeton).

Lambton, A.K.S. (1995), 'Major-General Sir John Malcolm (1769-1833) and *The History of Persia*', *Iran* 33, 97-109.

Lane Fox, R. (2006) 'The letter to Gadatas', in G. Malouchou and A.P. Matthaiou (eds) *XIAKON SUMPOSION EIS MNEMEN W.G. Forrest* (Athens), 149-71.

Lane Fox, R. (2007) 'Alexander the Great: "Last of the Achaemenids"?', in C.J. Tuplin (ed.) *Persian Responses: Political and Cultural Interaction with(in) the Achaemenid Empire* (Swansea), 267-311.

Lanfranchi, G., M. Roaf and R. Rollinger (eds) (2003) *Continuity of Empires (?): Assyria, Media, Persia* (Padua).

Lang, M. (1972) 'War and the rape-motif, or why did Cambyses invade Egypt?', *Proceedings of the American Philosophical Society* 116, 410-14.

Lecoq, P. (1997) *Les inscriptions de la Perse achéménide* (Paris).

Lenfant, D. (1996) 'Ctésias et Hérodote, ou les réécritures de l'histoire dans la Perse achéménide', *Revue des études grecques* 109, 348-80.

Lenfant, D. (2001) 'La "decadence" du Grand Roi et les ambitions de Cyrus le Jeune: aux sources perses d'un mythe occidental?', *Revue des études grecques* 114, 407-38.

Lenfant, D. (2004) *Ctésias de Cnide. La Perse. L'Inde. Autres fragments* (Paris).

Lenfant, D. (2007) 'On Persian *tryphê* in Athenaeus', in C.J. Tuplin (ed.) *Persian Responses: Political and Cultural Interaction with(in) the Achaemenid Empire* (Swansea), 51-65.

Lenfant, D. (2009) *Les Histoires Perses de Dinon et d'Héraclide* (Persika 13, Paris).

Lewis, D.M. (1977) *Sparta and Persia* (Leiden).

Lewis, D.M. (1985) 'Persians in Herodotus', in M.H. Jameson (ed.) *The Greek Historians: Papers ... A.E. Raubitschek* (Palo Alto), 89-115, repr. in his *Selected Papers in Greek and Near Eastern History* (ed. P.J. Rhodes, Cambridge), 345-61.

Lewis, D.M. (1987) 'The King's dinner', in A. Kuhrt and H. Sancisi-Weerdenburg (eds) *Achaemenid History II: The Greek Sources* (Leiden), 79-87, repr. in his *Selected Papers in Greek and Near Eastern History* (ed. P.J. Rhodes, Cambridge), 332-41.

Lewis, D.M. (1990) 'The Persepolis fortification texts', in H. Sancisi-Weerdenburg and A. Kuhrt (eds) *Achaemenid History IV: Centre and Periphery* (Leiden), 1-6, repr. in his *Selected Papers in Greek and Near Eastern History* (ed. P.J. Rhodes, Cambridge) 325-31.

Lewis, D.M. (1994) 'The Persepolis tablets: speech, seal and script', in A.K. Bowman and G. Woolf (eds) *Literacy and Power in the Ancient World* (Cambridge), 17-32.

173

Bibliography

Lewis, S. (1998) 'Who is Pythius the Lydian?', *Histos* 2, http://www.dur.ac.uk/Classics/histos/1998/lewis.html.

Lewis, S. (2002) *The Athenian Woman: An Iconographic Handbook* (London).

Lianieri, A. (2007) 'The Persian wars as the "origin" of historiography: ancient and modern Orientalism in George Grote's *History of Greece*', in E. Bridges, E. Hall and P.J. Rhodes (eds) *Cultural Responses to the Persian Wars: Antiquity to the Third Millennium* (Oxford), 331-53.

Lincoln, B. (2007) *Religion, Empire and Torture: The Case of Achaemenian Persia, With a Postscript on Abu Ghraib* (Chicago).

Llewellyn-Jones, L. (2002) 'Eunuchs and the royal harem in Achaemenid Persia (559-331 BC)', in S. Tougher (ed.) *Eunuchs in Antiquity and Beyond* (London), 19-49.

Llewellyn-Jones, L. (2003) *Aphrodite's Tortoise: The Veiled Woman of Ancient Greece* (Swansea).

Llewellyn-Jones, L. and J. Robson (2010) *Ctesias' History of Persia. Tales of the Orient* (London).

Lloyd, A.B. (1982) 'The inscription of Udjahorresnet. A collaborator's testament', *Journal of Egyptian Archaeology* 68, 168-80.

Lloyd, A.B. (1988) 'Herodotus on Cambyses: some thoughts on recent work', in A. Kuhrt and H. Sancisi-Weerdenburg (eds.) *Achaemenid History III: Method and Theory* (Leiden), 55-66.

Lloyd, A.B. (2007) 'Darius I in Egypt: Suez and Hibis', in C.J. Tuplin (ed.) *Persian Responses: Political and Cultural Interaction with(in) the Achaemenid Empire* (Swansea), 99-115.

Luraghi, N. (2001) 'Local knowledge in Herodotus' *Histories*', in N. Luraghi (ed.) *The Historian's Craft in the Age of Herodotus* (Oxford), 138-60.

Ma, J. (2003) 'Kings', in A. Erskine (ed.) *A Companion to the Hellenistic World* (Oxford), 177-95.

Malandra, W.W. (2008) 'A.V. Williams Jackson', *Encyclopaedia Iranica* 14, 318-23.

Malcolm, J. (1815) *A History of Persia* (2 vols, London).

Malcolm, J. (1827) *Sketches of Persia* (published anonymously in 2 vols, London).

Marchand, S. (2009) *German Orientalism in the Age of Empire. Religion, Race, and Scholarship* (Cambridge).

Marincola, J. (2007) 'The Persian wars in fourth-century oratory and historiography', in E. Bridges, E. Hall, and P.J. Rhodes (eds) *Cultural Responses to the Persian Wars: Antiquity to the Third Millennium* (Oxford), 105-25.

Martorelli, A. (1977) 'Storia persiana in Erodoto: echi di versioni ufficiali', *Istituto Lombardo. Rendiconti (Classe di lettere e scienzi morali e storichei)* 111, 115-25.

Masson, O. (1950) 'A propos d'un rituel hittite pour la lustration d'une armée', *Revue de l'histoire des religions* 137, 5-25.

Bibliography

Meier, M., B. Patzek, U. Walter and J. Wiesehöfer (2004) *Deiokes, König der Meder. Eine Herodot-Episode in ihren Kontexten* (Oriens et Occidens 7, Stuttgart).

Meiggs, R. and D.M. Lewis (1988) *A Selection of Greek Historical Inscriptions to the End of the Fifth Century BC* (revised edn, Oxford).

Merritt-Hawkes, O.A. (1935) *Persia: Romance and Reality* (London).

Miller, M.C. (1997) *Athens and Persia in the Fifth Century: A Study in Cultural Receptivity* (Cambridge).

Millspaugh, A.C. (1925) *The American Task in Persia* (New York and London).

Moles, J. (1993) 'Truth and untruth in Herodotus and Thucydides', in C. Gill and T.P. Wiseman (eds) *Lies and Fiction in the Ancient World* (Exeter), 88-121.

Momigliano, A. (1975) *Alien Wisdom: The Limits of Hellenization* (Cambridge).

Moore, B.B. (1915) *From Moscow to the Persian Gulf. Being the Journal of a Disenchanted Traveller in Turkestan and Persia* (New York).

Morier, J.J. (1816) *A Journey through Persia, Armenia and Asia Minor to Constantinople in the years 1808 and 1809* (Philadelphia).

Morier, J.J. (1824) *The Adventures of Hajji Baba of Ispahan in England* (3 vols, London).

Morton, R.S. (1940) *A Doctor's Holiday in Iran* (New York & London).

Mounsey, A.H. (1872) *A Journey through the Caucasus and the Interior of Persia* (London).

Mousavi, A. (2003) 'Persepolis in retrospect: histories of discovery and archaeological exploration at the ruins of ancient Parseh', in M.C. Root (ed.) *Medes and Persians: Reflections on Elusive Empires. Ars Orientalis* 32 (2002), 209-51.

Moyer, I.S. (2002) 'Herodotus and an Egyptian mirage: the genealogies of the Theban priests', *Journal of Hellenic Studies* 122, 70-90.

Munson, R.V. (2001) *Telling Wonders: Ethnographic and Political Discourse in the Work of Herodotus* (Ann Arbor).

Munson, R.V. (2009) 'Who are Herodotus' Persians?', *Classical World* 102, 457-70.

Murray, O. (1987) 'Herodotus and oral history', in H. Sancisi-Weerdenburg and A. Kuhrt (eds) *Achaemenid History II: The Greek Sources* (Leiden), 93-115, repr. in N. Luraghi (ed.) *The Historian's Craft in the Age of Herodotus* (Oxford, 2001), 16-44.

Murray, O. (1988) 'The Ionian revolt', *Cambridge Ancient History*, vol. IV (2nd edn, Cambridge) 461-90.

Nawotka, K. (2003) 'Alexander the Great in Persepolis', *Acta Antiqua Academiae Scientiarum Hungaricae* 43, 67-76.

Nylander, C. (1970) *Ionians in Pasargadae* (Uppsala).

Nylander, C. (1979) 'Achaemenid imperial art', in M. Trolle Larsen (ed.) *Power and Propaganda: A Symposium on Ancient Empires* (Copenhagen Studies in Assyriology 7, Copenhagen), 345-59.

Bibliography

Nylander, C. (1993) 'Darius III, the coward king: point and counterpoint', in J. Carlsen (ed.), *Alexander the Great: Reality and Myth* (Analecta Romana Instituti Danici, Supplementum 21) (Rome), 145-59.

Olmstead, A.T. (1938) 'Persia and the Greek frontier problem', *Classical Philology* 34, 305-22.

Olmstead, A.T. (1948) *History of the Persian Empire* (Chicago).

Ouseley, W. (1819-23) *Travels in various countries of the East; more particularly Persia* (3 vols, London).

Pagden, A. (2008) *Worlds at War: The 2,500 Year Struggle between East and West* (Oxford).

Palagia, O. (2008) 'The marble of the Persephone from Persepolis and its historical implications', in S.M.R. Darbandi and A. Zournatzi (eds) *Ancient Greece and Ancient Iran: Cross-cultural Encounters* (Athens), 223-37.

Panaino, A. (2003) 'Herodotus I, 96-101: Deioces' conquest of power and the foundation of sacred royalty', in G. Lanfranchi, M. Roaf and R. Rollinger (eds) *Continuity of Empires(?): Assyria, Medea, Persia* (Padua), 327-38.

Parker, R. (1983) *Miasma: Pollution and Purification in Early Greek Religion* (Oxford).

Parker, R. (2004) 'Sacrificing twice seven children: Queen Amestris' exchange with the God under the Earth (7.114)', in I. Taifacos and V. Karageorghis (eds) *The World of Herodotus* (Nicosia), 151-7.

Parpola, S. (2003) 'Assyria's expansion in the 8th and 7th centuries and its long-term repercussions in the west', in W.G. Dever and S. Gitin (eds) *Symbiosis, Symbolism and the Power of the Past* (Winona Lake), 99-111.

Petit, T. (1993) 'Synchronie et diachronie chez les historiens de l'empire achéménide. A propos de deux ouvrages de M.A. Dandamaev', *Topoi Orient-Occident* 3/1, 39-71.

Pope, A.U. (1938) 'The significance of Persian art', in A.U. Pope (ed.) *A Survey of Persian Art: From Prehistoric Times to the Present*, vol. 1 (London and New York), 1-41.

Posener, G. (1936) *La première domination perse en Egypte* (Cairo).

Potts, D. (2005) 'Cyrus the Great and the kingdom of Anshan', in V.S. Curtis and S. Stewart (eds) *Birth of the Persian Empire* (London), 7-28.

Price, S. and L. Nixon (1990) 'The size and resources of Greek cities', in O. Murray and S. Price (eds), *The Greek City: From Homer to Alexander* (Oxford), 137-70.

Price, W. (1832) *Journal of the British Embassy to Persia; embellished with numerous views taken in India and Persia: also a dissertation upon the antiquities of Persepolis* (2nd edn, London).

Pritchett, W.K. (1993) *The Liar School of Herodotus* (Amsterdam).

Raaflaub, K. (2003) *The Discovery of Freedom in Ancient Greece* (rev. edn, Chicago).

Raimond, E.A. (2007) 'Hellenization and Lycian cults during the Achaemenid period', in C.J. Tuplin (ed.) *Persian Responses: Political and Cultural Interaction with(in) the Achaemenid Empire* (Swansea) 143-62.

Rawlinson, G. (1885) *The Seven Great Monarchies of the Ancient Eastern World* (New York).

Rawlinson, G. (1898) *Memoir of Major-General Sir Henry Creswicke Rawlinson* (London, New York, Bombay).

Rawlinson, H.C. (1846) *The Persian Cuneiform Inscription at Behistun* (London).

Ray, J.D. (1987) 'Egypt: dependence and independence (425-343 BC)', in H. Sancisi-Weerdenburg (ed.) *Achaemenid History I: Sources, Structures and Synthesis* (Leiden), 80-95.

Razmjou, S. (2003) 'Assessing the damage: notes on the life and demise of the statue of Darius from Susa', in M.C. Root (ed.) *Medes and Persians: Reflections on Elusive Empires. Ars Orientalis* 32 (2002), 81-104.

Razmjou, S. (2005) 'Ernst Herzfeld and the study of graffiti at Persepolis', in A.C. Gunter and S. Hauser (eds) *Ernst Herzfeld and the Development of Near Eastern Studies 1900-1950* (Leiden), 315-41.

Razmjou, S. (2008) 'Persia and Greece: a forgotten history of cultural relations', in S.M.R. Darbandi and A. Zournatzi (eds) *Ancient Greece and Ancient Iran: Cross-cultural Encounters* (Athens), 373-4.

Razmjou, S. (2010) 'Persepolis: a reinterpretation of palaces and their function', in J. Curtis and St.-J. Simpson (eds) *The World of Achaemenid Persia: History, Art and Society in Iran and the Ancient Near East* (London), 231-45.

Redfield, J. (1985) 'Herodotus the tourist', *Classical Philology* 80, 97-118.

Rhodes, P.J. (2007) 'The impact of the Persian wars on classical Greece', in E. Bridges, E. Hall and P.J. Rhodes (eds) *Cultural Responses to the Persian Wars: Antiquity to the Third Millennium* (Oxford), 31-45.

Rice, C.C. (1916) *Mary Bird in Persia*, with a foreword by the Rt Rev. C.H. Stileman (London).

Richter, G. (1946) 'Greeks in Persia', *American Journal of Archaeology* 50 (1946), 15-30.

Richter, G. (1949) *Archaic Greek Art against its Historical Background* (New York).

Roaf, M. (1983) *Sculptures and Sculptors at Persepolis, Iran* 21 (London).

Roaf, M. (1990) 'Sculptors and designers at Persepolis', in A.C. Gunter (ed.) *Investigating Artistic Environments in the Ancient Near East* (Washington DC), 105-14.

Roaf, M. (1998) 'Persepolitan echoes in Sasanian architecture: did the Sasanians attempt to re-create the Achaemenid empire?', in V.S. Curtis, R. Hillenbrand and J.M. Rogers (eds) *The Art and Archaeology of Ancient Persia: New Light on the Parthian and Sasanian Empires* (London), 1-7.

Roaf, M. (2010) 'The role of the Medes in the architecture of the Achaemenids', in J. Curtis and St.-J. Simpson (eds) *The World of Achaemenid*

177

Persia: History, Art and Society in Iran and the Ancient Near East (London), 247-53.

Rollinger, R. (1993) *Herodots babylonischer Logos: eine kritische Untersuchung der Glaubwürdigkeitsdiskussion* (Innsbruck).

Rollinger, R. (2000) 'Herodotus and the intellectual heritage of the ancient Near East', in S. Aro and R.M. Whiting (eds) *The Heirs of Assyria: Proceedings of the Opening Symposium of the Assyrian and Babylonian Intellectual Heritage Project* (Helsinki), 65-83.

Rollinger, R. (2004) 'Herodotus, human violence and the Ancient Near East', in I. Taifacos and V. Karageorghis (eds) *The World of Herodotus* (Nicosia), 121-50.

Rollinger, R. (2006) '"Griechen" und "Perser" im 5. und 4. Jahrhundert c. Chr. im Blickwinkel orientalischer Quellen *oder* Das Mittelmeer als Brücke zwischen Ost und West', in B. Burtscher-Bechter, P.W. Haider, B. Mertz-Baumgartner and R. Rollinger (eds) *Grenzen und Entgrenzungen: Historische und kulturwissenschaftliche überlegungen am Beispiel des Mittelmeerraums* (Würzburg), 125-52.

Rood, T. (1998) *Thucydides: Narrative and Explanation* (Oxford).

Root, M.C. (1979) *The King and Kingship in Achaemenid Art: Essays in the Creation of an Iconography of Empire* (Leiden).

Root, M.C. (1980) 'The Persepolis perplex: some prospects borne of retrospect', in D. Schmandt-Besserat (ed.) *Ancient Persia: The Art of an Empire* (Malibu), 5-13.

Root, M.C. (1985) 'The Parthenon frieze and the Apadana reliefs at Persepolis: reassessing a programmatic relationship', *American Journal of Archaeology* 89, 103-20.

Root, M.C. (1990) 'Circles of artistic programming: strategies for studying creative process at Persepolis', in A.C. Gunter (ed.) *Investigating Artistic Environments in the Ancient Near East* (Washington DC), 115-39.

Root., M.C. (1991) 'From the heart: powerful persianisms in the art of the western empire', in H. Sancisi-Weerdenburg and A. Kuhrt (eds) *Achaemenid History VI: Asia Minor and Egypt: Old Cultures in a New Empire* (Leiden), 1-29.

Root, M.C. (1997) 'Cultural pluralism on the Persepolis fortification tablets', *Topoi* Supplement 1, 229-52.

Root, M.C. (2003) 'The lioness of Elam: politics and dynastic fecundity at Persepolis', in W. Henkelman and A. Kuhrt (eds) *Achaemenid History XIII: A Persian Perspective. Essays in memory of Heleen Sancisi-Weerdenburg* (Leiden), 9-32.

Root, M.C. (2007) 'Reading Persepolis in Greek: gifts of the Yauna', in C.J. Tuplin (ed.) *Persian Responses: Political and Cultural Interaction with(in) the Achaemenid Empire* (Swansea), 177-224.

Root, M.C. (2008) 'Reading Persepolis in Greek – Part Two: marriage metaphors and unmanly virtues', in S.M.R. Darbandi and A. Zournatzi (eds) *Ancient Greece and Ancient Iran: Cross-cultural Encounters* (Athens), 195-219.

Ross, E. Denison (1931) *The Persians* (Oxford).

Sackville-West, V. (1926) *Passenger to Teheran* (London).

Said, E.W. (1978) *Orientalism* (New York).

Saïd, S. (2002) 'Greeks and Barbarians in Euripides' tragedies: the end of difference?' (tr. A. Nevill) in T. Harrison (ed.) *Greeks and Barbarians* (Edinburgh), 62-100, originally published (in French) in *Ktema* 9 (1984), 27-53.

Sancisi-Weerdenburg, H. (1980a) *Yauna en Persai: Grieken en Perzen in een ander perspectief* (Groningen).

Sancisi-Weerdenburg, H. (1980b) 'Colloquium Early Achaemenid History', *Persica* 9, 231-2.

Sancisi-Weerdenburg, H. (1982) 'Colloquium Early Achaemenid History', *Persica* 10, 274-84.

Sancisi-Weerdenburg, H. (1983) 'Exit Atossa: images of women in Greek historiography on Persia', in A. Cameron and A. Kuhrt (eds) *Images of Women in Antiquity* (London), 20-33.

Sancisi-Weerdenburg, H. (1984) 'Achaemenid History Workshop', *Persica* 11, 185-96.

Sancisi-Weerdenburg, H. (1985) 'The death of Cyrus: Xenophon's *Cyropaedia* as a source for Iranian history', in A.D.H. Bivar (ed.) *Papers in Honour of Professor Mary Boyce*, vol. II (Leiden), 459-72.

Sancisi-Weerdenburg, H. (1987a) 'Introduction', in H. Sancisi-Weerdenburg (ed.) *Achaemenid History I: Sources, Structures and Syntheses* (Leiden), xi-xiv.

Sancisi-Weerdenburg, H (1987b) 'Decadence in the empire or decadence in the sources? From sources to synthesis: Ctesias', in H. Sancisi-Weerdenburg (ed.) *Achaemenid History I: Sources, Structures and Synthesis* (Leiden), 33-45.

Sancisi-Weerdenburg, H. (1987c) 'The fifth oriental monarchy and hellenocentrism: Cyropaedia VIII viii and its influence', in H. Sancisi-Weerdenburg and A. Kuhrt (eds) *Achaemenid History II: The Greek Sources* (Leiden), 117-31.

Sancisi-Weerdenburg, H. (1987d) review of Cook 1983, *Bibliotheca Orientalis* 44, 489-95.

Sancisi-Weerdenburg, H. (1988a) ' "*Persikon de karta ho stratos dôron*": a typically Persian gift (HDT. IX 109)', *Historia* 37, 372-4.

Sancisi-Weerdenburg, H. (1988b) 'Was there ever a Median empire?' in A. Kuhrt and H. Sancisi-Weerdenburg (eds) *Achaemenid History III: Method and Theory* (Leiden), 197-212.

Sancisi-Weerdenburg, H. (1989a) 'The personality of Xerxes, king of kings', in L. De Meyer and E. Haerinck (eds) *Archaeologia Iranica et Orientalia, Miscellanea in honorem Louis Vanden Berghe* (Ghent), 549-62, repr. in

Bibliography

E.J. Bakker, I.J.F. de Jong and H. van Wees (eds) *Brill's Companion to Herodotus* (Leiden, 2002), 579-90.

Sancisi-Weerdenburg, H. (1989b) 'Gifts in the Persian empire', in P. Briant and C. Herrenschmidt (eds) *Le tribut dans l'empire perse* (Paris), 129-45.

Sancisi-Weerdenburg, H. (1990a) 'Achaemenid history: from hellenocentrism to Iranocentrism', in G. Gnoli and A. Panaino (eds) *Proceedings of the First European Conference of Iranian Studies, I: Old and Middle Iranian Studies* (Rome), 253-59.

Sancisi-Weerdenburg, H. (1990b) 'The quest for an elusive empire', in H. Sancisi-Weerdenburg and A. Kuhrt (eds) *Achaemenid History IV: Centre and Periphery* (Leiden), 263-74.

Sancisi-Weerdenburg, H. (1991) 'Nowruz in Persepolis', in H. Sancisi-Weerdenburg and J.W. Drijvers (eds) *Achaemenid History VII: Through Travellers' Eyes* (Leiden), 173-201.

Sancisi-Weerdenburg, H. (1993a) 'Alexander and Persepolis', in J. Carlsen (ed.), *Alexander the Great: Reality and Myth* (Analecta Romana Instituti Danici, Supplementum 21) (Rome), 177-88.

Sancisi-Weerdenburg, H. (1993b) 'Political concepts in Old Persian inscriptions', in K. Raaflaub (ed.) *Anfänge politischen Denkens in der Antike: die nahöstlichen Kulturen und die Griechen* (Munich), 145-63, 379-81, 382-3, 407, 423-4.

Sancisi-Weerdenburg (1993c) review of Hall 1989, *Mnemosyne* 46, 126-32.

Sancisi-Weerdenburg, H. (1994a) 'The construction and the distribution of an ideology in the Achaemenid empire', in M. van Bakel, R. Hagesteijn and P. van de Velde (eds) *Pivot Politics: Changing Cultural Identities in Early State Formation Processes* (Amsterdam), 101-19.

Sancisi-Weerdenburg, H. (1994b) 'The orality of Herodotus' *Medikos Logos* or: the Median empire revisited', in H. Sancisi-Weerdenburg, A. Kuhrt and M.C. Root (eds) *Achaemenid History VIII: Continuity and Change* (Leiden), 39-55.

Sancisi-Weerdenburg, H. (1995a) 'Darius I and the Persian Empire', in J. Sasson (with J. Baines, G. Beckman, K.S. Robinson) (eds) *Civilisations of the Ancient Near East* (New York), 2.1035-50.

Sancisi-Weerdenburg, H. (1995b) 'Persian food: stereotypes and political identity', in J. Wilkins, D. Harvey and M. Dobson (eds) *Food in Antiquity* (Exeter), 286-302.

Sancisi-Weerdenburg, H. (1996) 'Darius II', *Encyclopaedia Iranica* 7, 50-1.

Sancisi-Weerdenburg, H. (1997) 'Crumbs from the royal table. Foodnotes on Briant (pp. 297-306)', *Topoi* Supplement 1, 333-45.

Sancisi-Weerdenburg, H. (1999) 'The Persian king and history', in C.S. Kraus (ed.) *The Limits of Historiography: Genre and Narrative in Ancient Historical Texts* (Leiden), 91-112.

Sancisi-Weerdenburg, H. (ed.) (2000) *Peisistratos and the Tyranny: A Reappraisal of the Evidence* (Amsterdam).

Sancisi-Weerdenburg, H. (2001a) 'Yauna by the sea and those across the sea', in I. Malkin (ed.) *Ancient Perceptions of Greek Ethnicity* (Washington DC), 323-46.

Sancisi-Weerdenburg, H. (2001b) 'The problem of the Yauna', in R. Bakir (ed.) *Achaemenid Anatolia. Proceedings of the First International Symposium on Anatolia in the Achaemenid Period* (Leiden), 1-11.

Sancisi-Weerdenburg, H. and J.W. Drijvers (1991) 'Introduction', in H. Sancisi-Weerdenburg and J.W. Drijvers (eds) *Achaemenid History VII: Through Travellers' Eyes* (Leiden), ix-xii.

Sancisi-Weerdenburg, H., A. Kuhrt and M.C. Root (eds) (1994) *Achaemenid History VIII: Continuity and Change* (Leiden).

Shahbazi, A.S. (2003) 'Irano-Hellenic notes 3: Iranians and Alexander', *American Journal of Ancient History* 2, 5-38.

Shahbazi, A.S. (2004) 'Harem I in ancient Iran', *Encyclopaedia Iranica* 12.1-3.

Simpson, St. J. (2003) 'From Persepolis to Babylon and Nineveh: the rediscovery of the ancient Near East', in K. Sloan (ed.) *Enlightenment: Discovering the World in the Eighteenth Century* (London), 192-201.

Smelik, K.A.D. (1978/9) 'The "omina mortis" in the Histories of Alexander the Great', *Talanta* 10/11, 92-111.

Sourvinou-Inwood, C. (1991) *'Reading' Greek Culture: Texts and Images, Rituals and Myths* (Oxford).

Spycket, A. (1980) 'Women in Persian art', in D. Schmandt-Besserat (ed.) *Ancient Persia: The Art of an Empire* (Malibu), 43-5.

Steiner, D. (1994) *The Tyrant's Writ: Myths and Images of Writing in Ancient Greece* (Princeton).

Stevenson, R.B. (1987) 'Lies and invention in Deinon's *Persica*', in H. Sancisi-Weerdenburg and A. Kuhrt (eds) *Achaemenid History II: The Greek Sources* (Leiden), 27-35.

Stevenson, R.B. (1997) *Persica* (Edinburgh).

Stewart, C.E. (1911) *Through Persia in Disguise: With Reminiscences of the Indian Mutiny*, edited from his diaries by Basil Stewart (London and New York).

Stolper, M. (1999) 'Une "vision dure" de l'Histoire Achéménide', *Annales HSS* 54.5, 1109-26.

Strauss, B.S. and J. Ober (1990) *The Anatomy of Error: Ancient Military Disasters and their Lessons for Modern Strategists* (New York).

Stronach, D. (1978) *Pasargadae: A Report on the Excavations Conducted by the British Institute of Persian Studies from 1961 to 1963* (Oxford).

Stronach, D. (1997a) 'Anshan and Parsa: Early Achaemenid history, art and architecture on the Iranian Plateau', in J. Curtis (ed.) *Mesopotamia and Iran in the Persian Period* (London), 35-53.

Stronach, D. (1997b) 'Darius at Pasargadae: a neglected source for the history of early Persia', *Topoi* Supplement 1, 351-63.

Stronk, J.P. (2007) 'Ctesias of Cnidus, a reappraisal', *Mnemosyne* 60, 25-58.

Sykes, E.C. (1898) *Through Persia on a Side-Saddle* (London).

Bibliography

Sykes, E.C. (1910) *Persia and its People* (London).

Sykes, P.M. (1902) *Ten Thousand Miles in Persia or Eight Years in Irán* (New York).

Sykes, P.M. (1915) *A History of Persia* (London).

Sykes, P.M. (1922) *Persia* (Oxford).

Thiers, C. (1995) 'Civils et militaires dans les temples. Occupation illicite et expulsion', *Bulletin de l'Institut Français d'Archéologie Orientale du Caire* 95, 493-516.

Thomas, R. (2000) *Herodotus in Context: Ethnography, Science and the Art of Persuasion* (Cambridge).

Tougher, S. (2008) *The Eunuch in Byzantine History and Society* (London).

Tuplin, C. (1987) 'The administration of the Achaemenid Empire', in I. Carradice (ed.), *Coinage and Administration in the Athenian and Persian Empires* (British Archaeological Reports 343, Oxford), 109-66.

Tuplin, C.J. (1990) 'Persian décor in *Cyropaedia*: some observations', in H. Sancisi-Weerdenburg and J.W. Drijvers (eds) *Achaemenid History V: The Roots of the European Tradition* (Leiden), 17-29.

Tuplin, C.J. (1991) 'Darius' Suez canal and Persian imperialism', in H. Sancisi-Weerdenburg and A. Kuhrt (eds) *Achaemenid History VI: Asia Minor and Egypt: Old Cultures in a New Empire* (Leiden), 237-83.

Tuplin, C.J. (1996) *Achaemenid Studies* (Stuttgart).

Tuplin, C.J. (1997a) 'Medism and its causes', *Transeuphratène* 13, 155-85.

Tuplin, C.J. (1997b) 'Achaemenid arithmetic: numerical problems in Persian history', *Topoi* Supplement 1, 365-421.

Tuplin, C.J. (2004) 'Doctoring the Persians: Ctesias of Cnidus, physician and historian', *Klio* 86, 305-47.

Tuplin, C.J. (2005) 'Darius' accession in (the) Media', in P. Bienkowski, C. Mee and E. Slater (eds) *Writing and Ancient Near Eastern Society* (New York), 217-44.

Tuplin, C.J. (2007) 'Introduction', in C.J. Tuplin (ed.) *Persian Responses: Political and Cultural Interaction with(in) the Achaemenid Empire* (Swansea), xiii-xxv.

Tuplin, C.J. (2008) 'The Seleucids and their Achaemenid predecessors: a Persian inheritance?', in S.M.R. Darbandi and A. Zournatzi (eds) *Ancient Greece and Ancient Iran: Cross-cultural Encounters* (Athens), 109-36.

Tuplin, C. (2009) 'The Gadatas Letter', in L.G. Mitchell and L. Rubinstein (eds) *Greek History and Epigraphy: Essays in Honour of P.J. Rhodes* (Swansea), 155-84.

Tuplin, C.J. (forthcoming, 2010) 'The limits of Persianization: some reflections on cultural links in the Persian empire', in E. Gruen (ed.) *Cultural Identity and the Peoples of the Ancient Mediterranean* (Los Angeles).

Unvala, J.M. (1938) 'Achaemenid architecture D. Some inscriptions', in A.U. Pope, (ed.) *A Survey of Persian Art: From Prehistoric Times to the Present*, vol. 1 (London and New York), 336-45.

van der Spek, R.J. (2003) 'Darius III, Alexander the Great and Babylonian scholarship', in W. Henkelman and A. Kuhrt (eds) *Achaemenid History XIII: A Persian Perspective. Essays in Memory of Heleen Sancisi-Weerdenburg* (Leiden), 289-346.

van der Veen, J.E. (1996) *The Significant and the Insignificant: Five Studies in Herodotus' View of History* (Amsterdam).

Vasunia, P. (2001) *The Gift of the Nile: Hellenizing Egypt from Aeschylus to Alexander* (Berkeley).

Vasunia, P. (2003) 'Hellenism and Empire: Reading Edward Said', *Parallax* 9, 88-97.

Vasunia, P. (2007) 'The philosopher's Zarathushtra', in C.J. Tuplin (ed.) *Persian Responses: Political and Cultural Interaction with(in) the Achaemenid Empire* (Swansea), 237-65.

Vernant, J.-P. (1962) *Les origines de la pensée grecque* (Paris), translated as *The Origins of Greek Thought* (Ithaca, 1982).

Wachtsmuth, F. (1938) 'Achaemenid architecture. A. The principal monuments', in A.U. Pope (ed.) *A Survey of Persian Art: From Prehistoric Times to the Present*, vol. 1 (London and New York), 309-20.

Waerzeggers, C. (2003/4) 'The Babylonian revolt against Xerxes and the "end of archives"', *Archiv für Orientforschung* 50, 150-73.

Walser, G. (1984) *Hellas und Iran: Studien zu den griechisch-persischen Beziehungen vor Alexander* (Darmstadt).

Waters, M. (1996) 'Darius and the Achaemenid line', *Ancient History Bulletin* 10, 11-18.

Waters, M. (2004) 'Cyrus and the Achaemenids', *Iran* 42, 91-102.

Waters, M. (2010) 'Cyrus and the Medes', in J. Curtis and St.-J. Simpson (eds) *The World of Achaemenid Persia: History, Art and Society in Iran and the Ancient Near East* (London), 63-71.

Weber, U. and J. Wiesehöfer (1996) *Das Reich der Achaimeniden: eine Bibliographie* (Berlin).

Weiskopf, M. (1989) *The So-Called 'Great Satraps' Revolt' 366-360 BC Concerning Local Instability in the Achaemenid Far West* (Stuttgart).

Weiskopf, M. (2008) 'The system Artaphernes-Mardonius as an example of imperial nostalgia', in S.M.R. Darbandi and A. Zournatzi (eds) *Ancient Greece and Ancient Iran: Cross-cultural Encounters* (Athens), 83-91.

West, S. (1987) 'And it came to pass that Pharaoh dreamed: notes on Herodotus 2.139, 141', *Classical Quarterly* 35, 262-71.

West, S. (2002) 'Demythologisation in Herodotus', *Xenia Toruniensia* 6 (Torun).

West, S. (2003) 'Croesus' second reprieve and other tales of the Persian court', *Classical Quarterly* 53, 416-37.

West, S. (2007) ' "Falsehood grew greatly in the land": Persian intrigue and Greek misconception', in R. Rollinger, A. Luther and J. Wiesehöfer (eds) *Getrennte Wege? Kommunikation, Raum und Wahrnehmung in der alten Welt* (Frankfurt am Main), 404-24.

Wiemer, H.-U. (2007) 'Alexander – der letzte Achaimenide? Eroberungs-

Bibliography

politik, locale Eliten, und altorientalische Traditionen im Jahr 323',
Historische Zeitschrift 284, 281-309.

Wiesehöfer, J. (1978) *Der Aufstand Gaumatas und die Anfänge Dareios I*
(Bonn).

Wiesehöfer, J. (1988) 'Das Bild der Achaeimeniden in der Zeit des
Nazionalsozialismus', in A. Kuhrt and H. Sancisi-Weerdenburg (eds)
Achaemenid History III: Method and Theory (Leiden) 1-14.

Wiesehöfer, J. (1996) *Ancient Persia*, tr. A. Azodi (London).

Wiesehöfer, J. (2003) '"Denn ihr huldigt nicht einem Menschen als eurem
Herrscher, sondern nur den Göttern": Bemerkungen zur Proskynese in
Iran', in C.G. Cereti, M. Maggi, and E. Provasi (eds) *Religious Themes
and Texts of Pre-Islamic Iran and Central Asia: Studies in Honour of
Professor Gherardo Gnoli on the occasion of his 65th Birthday on 6th
December 2002* (Wiesbaden), 447-52.

Wiesehöfer, J. (2004) '"O Master, remember the Athenians": Herodotus
and Persian foreign policy', in I. Taifacos and V. Karageorghis (eds) *The
World of Herodotus* (Nicosia), 209-21.

Wiesehöfer, J. (2006) '"Keeping the two sides equal": Thucydides, the
Persians, and the Peloponnesian war', in A. Rengakos and A. Tsakmakis
(eds) *Brill's Companion to Thucydides* (Leiden), 657-67.

Williams, E.C. (1907) *Across Persia* (London).

Woodman, A.J. (1988) *Rhetoric in Classical Historiography* (London).

Wright, D. (2001) *The English Amongst the Persians: Imperial Lives in
Nineteenth-Century Iran* (revised paperback edn, London).

Wynn, A. (2003) *Persia in the Great Game: Sir Percy Sykes: Explorer,
Consul, Soldier, Spy* (London).

Young, T.C. (1980) '480/479 BC – a Persian perspective', *Iranica Antiqua*
15, 213-39.

Index

Index

Index

Index

Index